PRAISE FOR *POWER CUES*

"Nick Morgan's ideas in *Power Cues* aren't just talk. They're the depth and pulse of what's missing when you ask why you're not more successful. This is your chance to fix that."
—Chris Brogan, CEO and Publisher, *Owner* magazine

"There are few skills more important in the twenty-first century than communicating with persuasion. Nick Morgan is a true master of this craft, with advice and insight honed in decades as a speaking coach. Read this engaging book and watch your impact soar."
—Pamela Slim, best-selling author, *Body of Work*

"I have to study body language every day when I negotiate with customers. *Power Cues* is the book I wish I'd had twenty years ago—I would have won a lot more negotiations and made a lot more money!"
—Les Gold, star of truTV's *Hardcore Pawn; New York Times* best-selling author, *For What It's Worth*

"Finally, a book that defines the importance of how the human form communicates. Morgan has researched how humans interact and provides practical, scientifically proven tips for communicating confidently with influence. Bravo!"
—Nancy Duarte, CEO, Duarte, Inc.; author, *HBR Guide to Persuasive Presentations*

"This is one of the most important books you will ever read. Not just this year—ever. There's an old saying that words account for only 7 percent of your communication. *Power Cues* covers the other 93 percent (and even some of the 7 percent). My hope is that everybody in the workforce today will read this book. More important, I wish that every student would be forced to read this book—or take a class with Nick Morgan."

—Mitch Joel, President, Twist Image; author, *Six Pixels of Separation* and *Ctrl Alt Delete*

"Wow! I wish I'd had this book ten years ago. Nick Morgan is a masterful communicator and teacher, and he has written another must-have book for anyone serious about greatly improving their interpersonal communication and leadership skills. A very helpful, informative, and engaging read—perfect for businesspeople, students, teachers, and beyond."

—Garr Reynolds, author, *Presentation Zen* and *The Naked Presenter*

POWER

CUES

POWER CUES

The Subtle Science of Leading Groups, Persuading Others, and Maximizing Your Personal Impact

NICK MORGAN

HARVARD BUSINESS REVIEW PRESS
BOSTON, MASSACHUSETTS

The web addresses referenced in this book were live and correct at the time of the
book's publication but may be subject to change.

Library of Congress Cataloging-in-Publication Data

Morgan, Nick.
   Power cues : the subtle science of leading groups, persuading others, and
maximizing your personal impact / Nick Morgan.
      pages cm
   ISBN 978-1-4221-9350-1 (alk. paper)
   1. Communication in management. 2. Interpersonal communication.
   3. Influence (Psychology) 4. Leadership. 1. Title.
   HD30.3.M665 2014
   658.4'5—dc23   2013050170

The paper used in this publication meets the requirements of the American
National Standard for Permanence of Paper for Publications and Documents in
Libraries and Archives Z39.48-1992.

ISBN: 9781422193501
eISBN: 9781422193600

i Nikki
Tri chynnig i Gymro

CONTENTS

INTRODUCTION

The Invisible Force That Rules
Human Interaction   1

CHAPTER ONE

Knowing Your Own Power Cues   23
Becoming Self-Aware and the Significance of Gesture

CHAPTER TWO

Taking Charge of Your Nonverbal
Communication   53
*Projecting Your Desired Persona—
through Your Emotions*

CHAPTER THREE

Reading the Unconscious Signals of Others   83
*How to Recognize and Understand
Emotional Cues in Gestures*

CHAPTER FOUR

Mastering Your Own Voice   119
The Most Powerful Leadership Cue

CHAPTER FIVE

Communicating as a Leader   145
Combining Voice and Body Language for Success

Contents

CHAPTER SIX

Using Your Intuition Effectively   175
*What Your Gut Is Really Saying —
and How to Leverage It*

CHAPTER SEVEN

Synchronizing Minds   201
How to Use Story to Get on the Same Wavelength

CONCLUSION

Community and Communication
Radical Authenticity   231

Notes   245
Index   251
Acknowledgments   259
About the Author   261

The Invisible Force That Rules Human Interaction

The Dalai Lama, My Father, and My Early Death

Three things happened to me when I was seventeen that turned out to have a significant effect on my interest in communications and, specifically, nonverbal communications, later in life. First, I read a book about the Dalai Lama and made him one of my personal heroes.[1] Second, I learned my father was gay. And third, I died.

Let me take those in order. I read a book about the Dalai Lama's escape into India from the Communists in 1959 and immediately cast him as one of my heroes in a pantheon that included Martin Luther King Jr., President John F. Kennedy, and the Beatles. I was excited, therefore, a half-dozen or so years later when I had the chance to hear the Dalai Lama speak at the University of Virginia, where I was a graduate student, and cheerfully queued up for a seat in the small auditorium.

The room was overflowing with devotees, local Buddhists, and the merely curious. There was an excited, impatient buzz—or at least as impatient as Buddhists get—and the Dalai Lama was late. He was an hour late when he finally took the stage, crossing to the middle of the space slowly, hunched over a little, dressed in his signature saffron robes, much smaller than I'd imagined.

I realized I was holding my breath as he crossed the stage. To my astonishment, when he finally reached the center of the space, he sat on the floor, bypassing the comfortable chair that had been provided. He arranged his robes. He looked at us.

Then he said . . . nothing. He just looked at us for one minute, saying nothing. Two minutes went by, and he was silent. Three minutes passed, and still His Holiness said nothing.

We were transfixed. Finally, he let out an unearthly laugh, high and spacey, like a child's "hahahahahahaha." He said, "I'd better say something really important, I've kept you waiting for so long."

After that, his speech was an anticlimax. There was something about the way he looked at us in silence, each person in turn, for those three minutes, that made a much deeper impression on everyone in the room than anything he could have said about the science of happiness.

Comparing notes afterward with other attendees, I learned that we all shared the feeling that he had touched us in some profound way. I wanted to know: What was it that passed between us? What was it about the Dalai Lama's silent gaze that was so profound?

More broadly, how did nonverbal communication work? How could one person transfix me with a look?

A Look That Changed Two People Forever

A look also forever changed my relationship with my father. And it took place in a nanosecond on Christmas day.

I'd rushed around attempting to buy him a present with my usual lack of success. He was a hard man to buy presents for; he didn't have many hobbies and divided his life rigorously between work and home. When he was at home, he did DIY projects or played the piano. But he wasn't the kind of man you'd buy a hammer for; his deep interests were artistic and literary. I couldn't afford to buy him a second piano, so I was looking for a book.

I finally found E. M. Forster's posthumously published novel *Maurice.*[2] This was the book that revealed his homosexuality, and so had been embargoed until his death. I was dimly aware of this back story, but it wasn't foremost in my mind.

I chose it, I imagined, because of its literary merit. Glad to have the chore accomplished, I thought no more about it. I wrapped up the book and put it under the Christmas tree.

On Christmas day, when my dad got around to opening it, he tore off the wrappings and gave me a very brief, startled look, before regaining his composure, saying thanks, and moving on to the next present. But in that momentary, startled glance, I saw suddenly, intuitively and finally, that he was gay. It wasn't a question; it was an answer—to a question I hadn't realized consciously that I had asked.

Nothing was said out loud, and it was ten more years until my dad came out to me deliberately, but I knew it in that look.

That a whole secret life could be revealed in one glance was astonishing to me. Humans didn't need words to tell each other things, even very deeply guarded, private things. How could this be? How could his unconscious mind speak to me that way without him being consciously aware of it?

Never Toboggan Alone

Later that eventful Christmas season when I was seventeen, I was tobogganing with a couple of friends on a cold, icy afternoon. The first run went smoothly, so with seventeen-year-old bravado, I said, "We didn't go fast enough." My friends suggested that perhaps I'd like to try a solo run, so I did.

I got a running start, jumped on the toboggan, and crashed headfirst into a tree on the second turn. I fractured my skull and was taken to Geisinger Medical Center in Danville, Pennsylvania. The neurosurgeons there operated on me for a subdural hematoma—a blood clot—that was putting pressure on my brain and causing intense pain.

I was in a coma for a few days and, at some point during that coma, I died briefly—for a total of about fifteen minutes. I came back to life, woke up, and asked the nurse, "Where am I?" because, despite the cliché, it was what I wanted to know first.

I think the doctor was relieved too, because my question meant that I was at least roughly intact, mentally.

As it turned out, I was alive, yes, but not everything was normal. Over the next several weeks, I noticed that something odd had happened to my mental processes. The world—or at least the people in it—had become distant and strange for me.

I couldn't figure out affect—intent—in other people. Their words seemed hollow. I couldn't tell what they were thinking or feeling. I knew I should be able to tell what was going on with other people, but I couldn't. Everyone around me seemed like automatons, robots, without the affect I was used to before the accident.

Something in me had switched off, and I had no idea what. It meant that people were suddenly complete mysteries to me. It was terrifying.

So I began to study body language consciously, in a deliberate and indeed panicked attempt to figure out what people were feeling, what their intent was, what they actually *meant*. I focused obsessively on gesture, facial expressions, posture, the ways people revealed tension in their arms and shoulders, the way they moved closer or further away from each other, their smiles and frowns—everything, in short, that I could see that might tell me something about what they were feeling.

Then, after a couple of months of agonized and largely unsuccessful efforts to read people, efforts that were making me more and more anxious and depressed, something switched on again. The part of my brain that read other people effortlessly, more or less, switched back on as mysteriously as it had switched off.

But the whole experience awakened in me a lifelong interest in body language, gesture, and the conscious effort to understand what other people took for granted, happy to pick up emotion and intent for the most part unconsciously.

Over the years, I've continued to study unconscious human behavior to try to understand how people actually communicate. My work, first in a university setting with public speaking and Shakespeare students, and then with clients over the past two decades, has given me a rich set of experiences in the practical implications of focusing on body language in order to make communication more effective and persuasive for leaders and future leaders in politics, education, business, and entertainment. More recently, startling advances in brain science have made it possible to have the beginnings of a rigorously tested and grounded understanding of this essential piece of human behavior.

Out of these experiences and from these advances in science, I have developed the seven-step process to communications mastery you'll find in this book. The integrated system is mine; the research that underpins it comes from many scientists around the world.

We're Not Aware of Our Most Important Activities

Most of our communication is indeed unconscious. Our conscious brains can handle something like forty bits of information a second. That sounds like a lot until you know that our unconscious minds can handle 11 million bits of information per second.[3] So we've evolved to push much of our behavior down to our unconscious minds because they can handle these important chores so much more powerfully and rapidly.

Within those constraints, by far the biggest activity the brain undertakes is handling visual input. Visual data can be as much as 10 million bits of information per second out of that 11 million.[4] Yet, despite all that computing power and effort, we don't see reality. What we "see" are the mental images our brains put up in response to the visual input. In essence, the brain gets the visual stimuli, then scans its data banks to find the closest approximate forms that correspond to the visual data. Our minds then offer that stored image as an interpretation of reality. That's what our brains think they see. For example, in a field of view in which most things are still and one thing is moving, the brain doesn't bother to get input on all the still stuff, just the moving item.[5]

This kind of triage of visual input has evolved to such an extent because it's essential to our basic survival. It's part of how we're able to act before our conscious minds realize exactly what's happening. For example, if something dangerous is thrown at you and you duck without thinking, getting out of the way a split second before it could hurt you, that's your unconscious mind at work. If you move at virtually the same instant and with the same gesture as someone you love, that's your unconscious mind at work. And if you get a suddenly powerful gut feeling that the person across from you is concealing an important feeling or piece of news, that's your unconscious mind at work.

In the first instance, the conscious mind would be too slow to react. In the second and third instances, you'd simply have a much harder time relating well with others.

Precisely because all of this mental activity is unconscious, we're not aware of it until it has already started to happen. Studies show, in fact, that we make most decisions *unconsciously* and only become aware of them *consciously* afterward, once we already start acting on that decision. The delay can be as long as nine seconds.[6]

In short, for most of the things that matter, your unconscious mind rules you, not the other way around.

That should disturb you.

The idea chips away at the sense of personal autonomy you have, the sense that you're a sentient being in charge of what you think and how you feel. And, what's most important, the sense that you're aware of what's going on with you and around you.

In fact, your unconscious mind is in charge. That part of you that you're aware of, that you think of as you, is a chip of ice on top of the tip of the proverbial iceberg that is a human being.

But what if you could learn to become aware of the important parts of this unconscious mental activity? What if you could learn to read it in others' minds? And what if you could control conversations, meetings, and all sorts of interactions among the people around you, using that conscious awareness of everyone's unconscious minds, including your own?

What if you could walk into a room and effortlessly (or apparently effortlessly) take charge of it? What if you could switch on charisma at will, making all heads swivel in your direction when you walk into that room? What if you could become the natural leader—the go-to person—of most of the groups that you join?

What if you could learn the essential power cues that will enable you to master virtually any situation where you want or need to be in control?

Would that be worth the effort?

Take Control of Your Communications Before Someone Else Does

That's what this book is about. I'm going to take you through seven important nonverbal power cues that will teach you how our communications really work, show you how to take control of your own communications, and help you learn to guide others'.

Power in human communications and relations is indeed determined largely by the interplay of our unconscious minds. Recent neuroscience has given us for the first time a clear understanding of how that unconscious interplay works. We can now identify a series of specific cues that people exchange with one another to determine how they relate to each other. These seven power cues, if mastered, will allow you to control your own communications and those of the people around you.

By the final chapter, you'll know how to literally synchronize others' brain waves with your own. Along the way, I'll talk through some of the brain science, where it's helpful, and the experiences of my clients, because their stories will illuminate what's possible and what has actually worked in the real world.

The Seven Power Cues

Let's get started. Here's a quick overview of the seven power cues that will help you signal that you're the leader of the tribe gathered around you. I'll begin each discussion of the individual power cues with a question that highlights the opportunity for strengthening your interpersonal communications.

The first power cue is all about self-awareness.
How do you show up when you walk into a room?

You need to begin to get some sense of how you inhabit space, what your characteristic gestures are, and how you affect others. So you're going to take inventory to find out what you're doing that's effective and what's not. How are you showing up in your conversations, your meetings, and your presentations?

In short, what's your persona when you connect with others? Are you powerful and commanding? Are you friendly and warm? Do people fear you, trust you, like you, avoid you, flock to you? What happens? Do you take charge or take a backseat? These are the sort of impressions you need to understand better in order to begin the process of turning into a charismatic version of yourself.

*The second power cue involves taking charge of
your nonverbal communications in order to project
the persona you want to project—through your
emotions. What emotions do you convey through
your body language for important moments,
conversations, meetings, and presentations?*

Most of us are not charismatic most of the time because we don't manage and focus our emotions. So we meet other people with a hundred things on our minds and a mixed bag of emotions, like our cluttered to-do lists. The result is muddle, not charisma. In step two, you'll begin the process of learning to manage and focus your emotions when you need to, thus taking charge of your nonverbal communications, your persona, and your charisma, to use it at will.

Because gesture does in some ways help determine thought, you will also spend some time understanding groups of gestures so that you can monitor how you're doing. In other words, sometimes it does help to fake it until you make it! Or more precisely, you can work from either the inside out, that is, from emotion to gesture, or the outside in, that is, from gesture to emotion. The two approaches complement one another.

*The third power cue helps you learn to read
others' unconscious messages. What unconscious
messages are you receiving from others?*

Because you're already an expert, but at an unconscious level, this step in particular is all about becoming aware of unconscious messages you're already sending yourself, making them conscious in specific ways and at specific times, and then making the new habits routine.

Because your skills at reading others involves intent—intent toward you—you'll learn to shape and phrase what you ask of your unconscious mind in that way. It's a matter of learning what specific polarities or pairs of questions to ask your unconscious mind.

In this way, you'll begin to be able to recognize and understand what others are thinking before they themselves know it, in many cases. That's because emotional attitudes and decisions are made unconsciously first, then gestured about, then brought to the conscious mind. You'll learn to see the attitude or decision at the gesture stage and, thus, before the other person is self-aware.

With the fourth power cue, on the mysteries of the human voice, you will turn your voice into a commanding instrument for taking charge of a room. Do you have a leadership voice?

The research on the voice is surprising and little known; it will give you an edge over your colleagues and competitors that you will be able to master with some weeks' practice.[7] What's important to note, however, is that individual responses to this step vary considerably. Some find it easy to take control of their voices; others, less musical, find it more difficult.

But the results can be powerful and life changing, if you undertake them carefully and thoroughly. Your voice is something you likely take for granted and rarely think about except when you have a cold, but it is one of the primary ways in which you connect with and influence people every day. Controlling your voice is worth the effort.

The fifth power cue teaches you how to combine your voice and a host of other social signals to greatly increase your success rate in pitches, meetings, sales situations, and the like. What honest signals do you send out in key work and social situations?

Researchers at MIT have discovered that, for example, the success of a venture capital pitch meeting can be predicted with astonishing accuracy by tracking a few aspects of body language.[8] You need to know what those are and learn how to use them to your advantage in high-stress, high-stakes situations.

As with the second power cue, either you can learn to control the gestures that signal these messages or you can control the emotions that control the gestures. As you work your way through the seven power cues, you'll find that while the idea of taking emotional control of your life may at first appear strange or daunting, in the long run, you'll find it by far the easier, more natural way to project powerful leadership and the communications that go with it.

The sixth power cue shows you how to use the power of your unconscious mind to make decisions, rid yourself of phobias and fears, and create a new, more successful persona. Is your unconscious mind holding you back or propelling you forward?

You'll apply insights top athletes have used for decades to your personal and work issues in order to redefine your approach to the world, as you wish to design it. You'll use these techniques to remove your unconscious story lines that say, "I always go blank under stress," or "I tend to choke when the boss is pressuring me to speak up," or "When I get in front of a crowd, I get nervous and can't seem to do my best." All it takes is a memory of a bad experience to throw you off your world-class game.

You'll work at replacing the mental maps that are currently holding you back with winning ones. If it all sounds too "New Age" to work, take comfort in knowing that the technique was developed by top Soviet researchers during the Cold War in an attempt to dominate the Olympics—and it worked. It garnered the Soviets an extraordinary number of gold medals. The results are real, even if the actions are all in your head.

Finally, the seventh power cue helps you put it all together to become a master storyteller who actually synchronizes brain waves with your listeners to enhance your natural leadership capacity, increase your charisma, and move others to action. Are you telling powerful stories?

Good storytelling creates a sense of anticipation in the reader's or viewer's mind, and the experience is a pleasurable one for the participants. We humans like that kind of anticipation and confirmation. It's part of our deep-seated desire for communal experiences and tribal connections.

Great leaders are great storytellers. These leaders know that they must tell powerful stories to engage and enlist their followers. They know that storytelling is the only effective way to create the kind of transmittal of ideas and values that allows a leader's message to be heard and carried out over time and with many people. They know that the best storytelling taps into deep patterns in the human brain so that the stories fulfill the needs and expectations of the listeners and also create the right sets of messages for the leader's agenda.

The last power cue in this process involves becoming one of those master storytellers and learning how to create stories that will convey the essence of your leadership, your mission, and your passion.

I will argue that powerful storytelling is the only possible road to the radical authenticity demanded of leaders. In our 24/7, warts and all, YouTubed world, leaders have to be willing to show up with an authenticity that goes well beyond anything demanded of leaders in the past. This book will help you on that road.

Take Your Time

These concepts are easy to master, but mastery of your unconscious communication systems takes time. After all, it took a million years of evolution to put all that activity management into your unconscious mind. Most of it should stay there, with good reason. The unconscious mind handles chores like regulating your breathing, heartbeat, and skin temperature, and that's a good thing. You don't want to have to think about all the stuff that keeps you alive and healthy.

The aspects of unconscious thinking that I'm describing have to do with your so-called intuition, your reading of others' attitudes, emotions, and intents, and your control of your own body language, broadly defined to include your voice and posture as well as your mannerisms and gestures. These aspects turn out to be the most important for communication.

They do take time to bring to the conscious mind, master, and then send back down to the unconscious mind for retrieval when you need to. These are not simple changes; you're reengineering a finely tuned, incredibly complex organism with more synapses and connections than there are stars in the Milky Way.[9]

If some parts turn out to be more challenging for you, then take it slowly. Make sure that you're comfortable with each power cue before you move on to the next. For the most part, each step builds on the ones before it. So practice each concept for a few weeks until you're comfortable with it and then move on to the next step.

Above all, don't rush the process. You need to get into the habit of listening to your own unconscious mind in ways you most likely haven't before, and that takes time and patience.

Let go of your preconceptions. Open up your thinking. It's time to get to know your own mind.

Alice Got Here Before You Did

Welcome to Wonderland. Most of what we think about the way people communicate is wrong, yet the reality is much stranger and more astonishing than we can even imagine.

A series of recent breakthroughs in science have overturned the accepted wisdom about how we express ourselves to others, how we interpret what they say to us, and how we decide whether or not to follow another's leadership. These scientific studies not only allow us to understand communication in a new way, but also reveal how to become much more persuasive and successful without changing a single word we say.

Take the following recent findings from brain research:

- You gesture *before* you think consciously about what you're doing.

- You have neurons that fire when you witness someone else experiencing an emotion—*and they give you the exact same emotion.*

- If you lose your ability to process emotion, you lose your ability *to remember or to decide anything.*

- You emit *low-frequency sounds* that align with the most powerful person near you through matching vocal tones.

- Your *measurable nonverbal signals* concerning your confidence in a negotiation predict success or failure far more accurately than the relative merits of your position or what you say.

- Neurons are distributed *throughout your body*, not just in your brain, including your heart and your gut.

- When you communicate with someone else, *the two of you align your brain patterns*, even if you don't agree with the other person.

Each of these findings is surprising, and some truly defy common sense.[10] I'll talk more about each one in the coming chapters. But taken together they add up to a very different view of how people actually communicate and what you should do to connect with other people powerfully and persuasively.

Our Important Communications Are neither Verbal nor Conscious

Here's the good news. If we can tap into the hidden power that these findings reveal, we can take charge in meetings, dominate groups, and speak in front of audiences with charisma and persuasive eloquence, no matter what the subject or the occasion. We can lead people through the unconscious communication power our *bodies* give us. We don't need words—well, only a little bit; mostly, we need gesture and sound.

With the right gestures and vocal tones, virtually anyone can take over a group and lead it, creating an instant tribe with herself at its head. We humans literally want to align our brain patterns through interpersonal communications, and we feel safest and happiest when we're doing so. You can master group dynamics with your voice, your hands, and your posture. You can learn how to shape, control, and prompt the natural, unconscious responses people have in groups. You can learn how to control your own unconscious mind so that it does your bidding.

You can jump-start your leadership and propel it to the next level with these techniques.

In sum, people crave leadership. In order to be the best leader possible, you need to align your *unconscious* power cues with your *conscious* content to be able to lead groups, persuade others, and maximize your personal impact. Then you need to find your tribe.

No one gets led anywhere they don't want to go. Machiavelli was wrong; leadership is not manipulation, not in the long run.[11] It's alignment, the leader with the group and the group with the leader. But you first have to maximize and focus your leadership strengths in order to be ready when your moment comes.

What Humans Really Want

At the heart of this book is a surprising truth, one that defies most of the previous thinking about body language. People have studied it as a way of reading others, gesture by gesture and, indeed, sometimes as a way of consciously sending secret messages to others—messages of control or sexual interest, perhaps. Most of those early attempts to understand body language are silly and primitive.[12]

Here's what is really going on. We humans are much more communal than we realize. It's something we've forgotten, as we tune in separately to our thousand channels of entertainment and news using devices that isolate us even as they offer pseudo-connections to the group through music or headlines or games. We only remember our communality when we get together as a group to hear a speech, attend a concert, or root for a sports franchise.

But when we get together in groups, we become a tribe again, and we instinctively want to have a leader. That's *your* chance to take control, consciously using the power of every-one's unconscious mind.

That's why an audience is so eager for a speaker to succeed, for example, and so disappointed when one fails. There's an opportunity that is squandered a thousand times a day in a thousand meeting rooms around the world. Instead of focusing on the group, the emotion, and the need for leadership, speakers think about PowerPoint and content. What a huge amount of wasted effort!

We create a leader to make us feel safe and to give us a group purpose or direction. Because, like a group of fish or birds or zebra, we need and want guidance. As you'll see, the unconscious signals that the speaker sends out to the audience must create trust and credibility or else the audience gives up, disappointed, and looks elsewhere for another leader.

These group activities satisfy deep cravings that developed during our early evolution in the cave. In our prelinguistic, less individualistic childhood as a species, we depended on one another for survival, and leadership was both essential and instinctive.[13]

When we lived in caves, we humans were a relatively frail, weak species, below some formidable foes in the food chain—woolly mammoths, saber-toothed tigers, and the rest of the menagerie. So we learned to respond instantly to one another in order to stay alive. We could read each other's emotions, and we could tell who was in charge, without a word being spoken.

Today, most of the dangers to which we were ready to respond then have gone away. But our cravings for leadership and connection remain. Where once we needed to react instantly to physical danger, now most of us face long-term tensions associated with jobs, relationships, and communities. Where once we needed to be ready to act quickly as a tribe to stand united against dangers, now our individual opinions matter more than our tribal loyalties. Where once we found comfort in group rituals around a dim, smoky fire in a cave, now many of us put on ear buds to connect emotionally with our fellow humans through recorded music. Indeed, recent research shows that we respond to new music much as we do to sex and drugs.[14] When the baby boomers talked about sex, drugs, and rock and roll, they were on to something.

With what you're learning from the brain scientists, you can begin immediately to make your own communications more effective and powerful by tapping into that ancient craving for connection. You can learn how to overcome shyness, how to increase your charisma a hundredfold, how to control a room, how to get your teenager under control, even how to cure yourself of recurring thoughts, habits, and dreams.

It's not just brain research. I have lots of practical experience in these techniques through work with clients over the past two decades. For example, I trained one woman, who had always been put down by men in her professional life, to change their perception of her and take charge of her career—without saying a word.

I worked with another person whose shyness was damaging his career and his marriage. He learned to become a more effective communicator at work and at home—and became a CFO.

I helped another client double his speaking fees by making a few small changes in the way he stood in front of an audience.

You'll learn that what the brain research shows actually happens when people communicate, and how you can use that understanding to become a new kind of persuasive, charismatic leader yourself. You can achieve the same kind of transformation that I have seen over and over again in my work with clients over the past two decades.

How to Read This Book

I've sought to make this book as easy as possible to read, given the sophisticated nature of the coaching. Each of the seven chapters describes a particular set of insights derived from my coaching work, supported by a breakthrough in brain research, and discusses the implications for leadership and communications. Each chapter also describes, in very practical terms, a power cue leading to personal communications mastery that builds on the cues before it and overall creates a complete program for your personal transformation. You can jump right to the power cues and skip the research, but I recommend studying it because of the insights it will give you into why people communicate the way they do. It will help you in your pursuit of communications mastery to understand how the brain works and what science is showing us about aspects of the human unconscious.

I've tried to anticipate as many of the questions you will naturally have as possible, and answer them in the descriptions of the steps and instructions for implementing them yourself. I've also added "field notes" at the end of each chapter that cover some of the issues that may arise as you start to put these ideas into action. Think of them as deeper dives into the practical side of this work.

It's important to understand that much of this brain research is still in its early stages, and as such I have only included discussion of work that I have personally found to be helpful and practical in my work with clients—a nonstatistical but nontrivial form of confirmation. Where it's relevant and helpful, I will share stories of my client work to illustrate how the steps work, what pitfalls to avoid, and what you need to focus on to achieve the best results.

This work is going to take some weeks, and it's not easy. It requires paying attention to aspects of your behavior and others' behavior that you've probably not thought consciously about before. But the results will be worth it. Personal mastery and an opportunity to change your leadership level await you.

When I say *mastery*, I don't mean manipulation. These power cues will actually show you how to deal more authentically with your colleagues, your family, your tribe. In seven chapters, you'll learn how to clear away all the unconscious messages you don't mean to be sending—and don't even realize you're sending—in order to strengthen the messages you *want* to communicate. You'll learn to show up as the best version of yourself instead of as a jumble of unconscious fears and distractions. You'll become more persuasive and more powerful *because* you'll become more authentically yourself.

When you're ready, take a deep breath and turn the page.

CHAPTER ONE

Knowing Your Own Power Cues

Becoming Self-Aware and the Significance of Gesture

This chapter will explore how gesture establishes and regulates relationships and communications on several levels. It will discuss the work of psychologist Susan Goldin-Meadow on helping children learn through gesture and the surprising insights into the importance of gesture that resulted from her work. And it will describe the first step in communications mastery: taking inventory of your own gestures to become self-aware.

Let's Rethink Our Communications

It's time to rethink how we communicate. We now have a much clearer understanding of what people are up to when they commune with one another. Thanks to significant advances in brain science, we can piece together most of what goes on when people attempt to inform, cajole, persuade, amuse, enlighten, control, tease, infuriate, impassion, or lead each other. We don't have the whole picture with complete certainty, of course, but we now have enough to go on.

We have enough to understand what it takes to get an accurate picture of your own communications profile, to inspire other people, to understand them better, to lead them, to persuade others, to captivate other people with charisma, and to share your vision by becoming a passionate storyteller. These are the specific mysteries of communications I'll be focusing on in this book. Each of the seven power cues are specifically chosen to help you in these areas.

Before starting, you need to let go of your current ideas about communications. Whether they've come from high school debate training, a college course in public speaking, something your mother told you, or just your common sense, most of what you think you know about communications is wrong.

For example, one common misconception is that when giving a speech, you should "tell 'em what you're going to say, tell 'em, and tell 'em what you said." Now, there's nothing wrong with repetition, but the problem is that the world has sped up since that advice first came down the communications grapevine, and we no longer have the patience to listen to something someone tells us three times.

When was the last time you paid attention when someone went through an agenda slide? You didn't, right? You were on your smartphone checking your email one last time. How about when a speaker says, "In conclusion, what I've covered today is . . ." You were back on the smartphone or packing up your stuff. (Of course, if you're really Type A, you paid attention only during the opening summary or the ending summary; the rest of the time you were surreptitiously doing email.)

The point is that that sort of bald repetition no longer works because it moves too slowly for us in our attention-deficit-disorder (ADD) world. Repetition has to be artful, disguised, or impassioned like Martin Luther King Jr.'s "I Have a Dream" speech for it to work on our harried minds today.

The Bad News about PowerPoint

Another misconception that I frequently hear as a speech coach is the idea that PowerPoint helps because all people are one of the following: visual, kinesthetic, or aural learners. Neither idea buried in this generally accepted, appalling misconception is true!

First of all, we're all visual learners.[1] As I indicated in the introduction, we can handle up to 10 million visual bits of information per second, far more than anything else our minds can process. We're also all kinesthetic and aural learners. We get information in those other ways, too. Just not as much. Of course, there are individual variations, but most of us are average, and that means we're mostly visual beings. Unlike, say, cats and dogs, which have vastly more developed senses of smell. For us, it's visual.

Second, PowerPoint doesn't help; it distracts. All the research on multitasking shows that we can't do it.[2] We first pay attention to one thing, and then another. Moreover, the research on how our brains process visual information, as I alluded to in the introduction, indicates that we don't actually see what's in front of us, but rather an approximation of it that our brain matches to reality based on its memory banks.

So what really happens when we're confronted in a meeting or a presentation with a speaker and a set of slides is that we look at the speaker—because we're inherently more interested in people than pictures—and when our attentions start to wander, then we look at the slides. Now, reading slides and looking at people occupy two different parts of our brain, and there's a lot of inefficiency in switching back and forth. So when we're looking at the speaker, we're getting one set of cues. When we look at the slides, we get another set. When we switch, we lose a bit of either information stream.

So the result is two incomplete sets of information. That's tiring and indeed annoying for us, so we get cranky and tune out.

That's what PowerPoint (and any similar slideware or presentation program) does. With some exceptions, it adds to our information load, overwhelming it even faster, and causing us to tune out.

Don't do it.

It's All about the Handshake, Isn't It?

You've probably been told a thousand times that any good meeting with someone new begins with a firm handshake. Now, there's nothing wrong with a firm handshake, but in fact the important part of a meeting has nothing to do with the handshake and everything to do with the attitude that you bring to the meeting.

Before you say anything or even reach the other person, you telegraph, with a thousand subtle cues, how you're feeling about yourself, and how you feel about the other person. Indeed, the relationship has largely already been set by the time you're close enough to shake hands. Hand shaking just seals the deal. How you stand, how you move your arms, what your posture conveys, the expression on your face, the way you're walking, and yes, what you're wearing all affect the relationship more powerfully than that poor overstressed handshake.

Finally, generalizing from all the bad communications classes you've taken and coaches you've worked with, there are no secret power gestures or ways to position your hands or face so that strong men salute, women swoon, and everyone runs to do your bidding.

Individual gestures simply aren't that powerful. Really. Let that one go. Lose the steepled fingers or the enigmatic smile or the T-bar move. None of those do much more than occupy your conscious mind a little too much, distracting you from what you should be thinking about.[3]

So it's time to let go of the old rules and learn what's really going on. Let's begin with those much misunderstood gestures.

Two Conversations at Once

Every communication is two conversations. The first conversation is the one you're aware of—the spoken content. The second conversation is the one that we're all unconscious experts on—the nonverbal one.[4]

When the two are aligned, you can pay attention to the words, because the body language supports the content and so you can hear it. But when the two are sending out different messages, you believe the body language every time. That's why it's important. The body language always trumps the spoken content.

Moreover, these two conversations always go together. They are so integral to one another that most people tend to gesture with their hands and face even when they're talking on the phone. Think about it. No one else can see them, yet they keep gesturing regardless. Why do they do it?

Is it just habit? No, there's a profound reason why people gesture when they attempt to communicate, even when they can't be seen.

We tend to think that the second conversation is merely an accompaniment to the first. We talk, and we wave our hands in the air, as a poor substitute or stand-in for content. We believe, if we ever think about it, that the gestures are just follow-ons: something to do with our hands, or something that clarifies the meaning, emphasizes whatever's being said, or helps keep the other person listening. Or something that follows the words, perhaps—a physical flourish to enhance our sometimes less-than-thrilling (spoken) content.

That's not what's going on. In fact, gesture can convey meaning independent of words.

Try the following experiment. Sit in a public place, say, a restaurant where the tables are close together and the conversation is lively. Sit with your back to a pair of people who are having one of those animated conversations. Listen hard. Try to get as much of it as you can.

You will be surprised at how hard it is to follow the conversation. You will hear broken phrases, agreement to something you haven't caught, simultaneous talking, abrupt changes of topic you weren't expecting (but, for some reason, the speakers were), and apparently incoherent exchanges of information. If it's an average, reasonably equal exchange, you will be astonished at how fragmentary and elusive the communication is.

Why is that? Because we communicate first with the gesture for some things, and only second with the word. Because the "second conversation" is really the first. For certain kinds of communications, indeed most of the ones we really care about, we communicate first with the gesture and second with the word.

What does that mean? It means that when people communicate topics of great importance to them, they gesture what they intend a split second before the word comes out.

Why should we care about that? Because it turns the commonsense way we think about word and gesture upside down, and because those interesting implications flow from that inversion of common sense.

Gesture comes first.

You can confirm this for yourself if you go back to that restaurant, this time keeping your eyes firmly trained on those two people in conversation and listening very closely. Focus especially on gestures that accompany the noun phrases.

How did you get there?

I took an airplane.

Let's say that's one of the exchanges you hear and see. Watch the gesture associated with the word *airplane*. Depending on the information being conveyed, the gesture will start before the entire sentence or just before the word *airplane* itself.

If there's strong attitude, such as, something like, *Of course I took an airplane; it's three thousand miles away over water. How else would I get there, you idiot?* then the gesture may convey all the emotional freight in the communiqué—all the *Of course it's three thousand miles away over water how else would I get there you idiot* part.

The person might shrug and turn her palms upward, while raising her eyebrows and looking hard at the interlocutor. She might shake her head and offer a half-smile. Those facial and hand gestures would get across all the emotional meaning she wished to convey to her friend. Maybe not in precisely those words, but close enough for both parties to get the message.

It's the nature of most of our communications that they unroll like this one; we use surprisingly few words and convey the emotional colors and tones of the conversation mostly through gesture.

The Language of Love

When two people know each other well, the words are even less important.

Why? Because when two people know each other well, gesture can take up a larger part of the communications between them. In this regard, gesture becomes a kind of shortcut that allows the two to alert one another to important shifts in the conversation or strong feelings or topics to avoid. When two lovers meet, for example, not the ones in movies who have just fallen in love, but those who have had an intimate relationship for a long time, a touch, a few murmured words, and a kiss may convey all that needs to be said about a day, a meeting, or an important issue that has been pending between them.

Love is expressed primarily through gesture. A look, an arch of the eyebrow, a touch, a kiss. You get the idea.

Many of our dialogues with others—and most of our important ones—take place nonverbally. Large portions of them are unconscious.

So gesture comes first, and it conveys most of the emotion that a communication intends. In addition to emotion, certain other basic things are conveyed. Relationships, spatial distances between people, physical motion and place in general, basic needs like food, shelter, sex, and so on—all of these are first gesture conversations, then only secondarily and later content conversations. Think of it as everything that a smart caveman and -woman would need to get along on a typical busy day defending the hearth, slaying woolly mammoths, raising the kids, and creating those cave paintings in the few minutes at the end of the day that a cave person can call his or her own.

What else is going on? Unconscious thought is faster and more efficient than conscious thought.

As a species, we're always trying to articulate our feelings and telling people to get in touch with them, and so on, but in fact our feelings are doing quite well unconsciously. Unconscious thought is faster and more efficient, and may have saved your life on more than one occasion. It's just that it isn't conscious.

Here's the next implication. Two people—or a leader and her audience—can have an unconscious communication, one that is entirely composed of gestures of various kinds, and only realize it consciously later on or not at all. The two conversations don't even have to be connected.

When I say every communication is two conversations, both verbal and nonverbal, I mean that precisely. They don't have to have an immediate, obvious connection. They often do, but they don't have to. Think about the exchange between two people where one is bearing very bad news to the other. The bearer may gesture strong signals of comfort, love, and solidarity while quietly stating the shattering news in a simple, unadorned way.

There, the two conversations, though of course connected, are proceeding along two parallel tracks, and it is easier to see how the gesture is not merely an afterthought to the words. That kind of communication usually begins with the reassuring gesture or the look, which is what alerts the recipient that bad news is coming.

Or think about when two people are carrying on a flirtation under the noses of their colleagues while talking about meeting second-quarter quotas, for example. There, the two conversations are unrelated, to the great private amusement of the flirters.

What Gestures Really Mean

We haven't always understood the importance of this second conversation. Not so long ago, scientists didn't study the gestures with which we humans accompany speech because they were considered meaningless and obviously less interesting than so-called "emblems"—gestures with specific meanings, like the peace sign or the upraised middle finger.

So scientists studied emblems and downplayed the importance of gestures, because they didn't consider them to be as thoughtful and important as those few gestures every culture has that are really hand signals—a kind of code.[5]

That approach hobbled scientific progress for most of the twentieth century, but researchers finally shook it off and came at gestures from the opposite direction: that they can have meaning, just not the same sort of coded meaning as words.

Now we understand that gestures actually precede conscious thought and can even shape and guide it.[6] So important is gesture that we find it hard to communicate if we are unable to gesture.[7] Try speaking for any length of time with your hands tied behind your back, either literally or figuratively. You'll find it surprisingly difficult.

Gestures are an essential part of the communications process, because they signal directly from your unconscious to everyone's else unconscious mind what you're thinking, how you're feeling, and what you're intending toward those other people.

The first thing we want to know when we see people coming toward us is, are they friend or foe? We unconsciously evaluate their stance, their posture, where they're putting their hands, and what they're doing with them, in order to ascertain with astonishing speed whether we're about to get a punch or a kiss.[8]

There are two essential points here. The first is that you're always signaling, and so is everyone else, about your intentions and feelings. The second point is that most of the time you don't pay conscious attention to all those signals—either the ones you're putting out or the ones others are sending to you. Your unconscious mind handles all that.

Why Gesture Matters

Our minds are constructed to attribute intent to the gestures, attitudes, and postures of other people. We've evolved to be able to do that effortlessly, for the most part, by pushing the activity down to our unconscious minds, which are faster and more powerful than our conscious minds. So that's a good thing.

Except when we want to *understand* what it is that we're reading so effortlessly. What we're actually doing is monitoring the thousands of minute adjustments in body language that the people around us are constantly making. They do so to express their unconscious attitudes, intents, and emotions. We do so in order to understand what they're saying. The whole process probably preceded our ability to vocalize as a species.

To understand why this counterintuitive situation might exist, it helps to learn a little about how the brain works. It's not what we think. Most of us have this idea that we can call the "Mr. Spock Theory of the Brain," after the *Star Trek* character known for his logic and ability to keep his emotions under control. So, for example, we imagine that we get a thought, such as, "I'm thirsty," and then we direct our bodies to act on that thirst, reaching for a glass of water. Neat, logical, and very Spockian.

But it turns out that our bodies don't work that way. What actually happens is that we get an unconscious intent or desire—like thirst—and then our bodies start acting on that intent or desire. Only after that—entire nanoseconds later—do our conscious minds catch on to what's happening. In effect, our conscious minds say, "I just noticed that I'm reaching for water. I must be thirsty. Yes, that's it. I'm thirsty. Good thing I've got a drink of water heading my way."[9]

That's counterintuitive, and it probably makes you a little uncomfortable. But that's the way it is. Our conscious minds are just along for the ride, like one of those birds that sits on a hippopotamus, picking off the bugs that swarm around the beast.

How Our Minds Really Work: Not So Much

We're barely in control of our simplest, most basic needs, let alone our higher-order wishes and desires. Again, one of the purposes of this book is to give you far more control over what's happening to you and your body as you go through your daily life.

Now, let's be clear that most of the time unconscious control of moments, like that of thirst, is a good thing. If you were aware of everything your unconscious mind took care of, from keeping your heart beating and your body temperature relatively constant to monitoring your surroundings for incoming hazards, you'd quickly be overwhelmed by the sheer tediousness of it all. There's a good reason why most of that stuff is run—beautifully—by your unconscious mind. It does it really, really well, so you don't have to.

That frees up your conscious mind for more interesting things and important moments. But the problem with the arrangement is that it leaves you largely helpless in those moments when you do want to take control of a room, a meeting, or a negotiation. You want to do it subtly, without everyone else becoming aware of your sudden wielding of power, because it's far more effective that way.

So what I'm going to do is to show you how to learn to become conscious of those aspects of your unconscious behavior that are most important for confidence, intuition, charisma, and leadership. You're going to learn to control them and then you'll be able to bring them to conscious awareness when you want to and leave them to your unconscious mind when you're not trying to take charge.

That's mastery. And it begins with the conscious control of your own hitherto unconscious gestures, and the conscious reading of others' gestures, something you have also left to your unconscious mind until now.

What the Research Says about Your Hands: They're Smarter Than You Think

Let's go a little deeper into the language and meaning of gesture and its use. You need to know what's really at stake. And it will surprise you.

Psychologist Susan Goldin-Meadow kept noticing something strange.[10] One of the prime tests psychologists use to determine how advanced a child is in her development is what is known as the "conservation test." This test has a child pour liquid from a tall, skinny glass into a squat, fat glass. Now, because the second glass is shorter in height, very young children will tell you that there is less water once they've poured it into the second glass.

But once a child reaches a certain point in her development, she realizes that the liquid is *conserved*—that it's the same amount. That's conservation, and it's an important breakthrough in everyone's development, as a child growing up.

Goldin-Meadow noticed that when you asked children to explain their rationale for figuring out whether the liquid is conserved or not, they gestured a lot. In fact, sometimes they gestured things that they didn't say. Kids who understood the concept might, for example, flip their hands back and forth to indicate that the two amounts of water were the same. Some of the kids who couldn't yet verbally explain the idea would also make that flipping gesture, as if their hands knew something their brains didn't.

This was surprising, because the dominant view about gesture until pioneers like Goldin-Meadow taught us differently was that gesture was a meaningless accompaniment to speech, which was really the important stuff.

You Don't Say What You Mean—You Gesture It

What Goldin-Meadow was noticing was that gesture and speech were different, and things were being said by the children with their gestures that they didn't say with their speech. As she notes, "It's hard even to think about gestures separately from speech. We (coded) them separately. So we'd code the speech without the picture, and then we'd turn the sound off and code the gesture." The accidental result was that Goldin-Meadow and her fellow researchers noticed that speech and gesture were not the same.

You don't normally notice this phenomenon in ordinary communication. As Goldin-Meadow says, "That's not how our brains process it. Our brains just glom it all together and integrate it." So it took an expert to notice that our gestures have meaning, and meaning different from what we're saying.

You don't notice this phenomenon consciously, but your unconscious mind is keeping track of it. Goldin-Meadow says, "We did some brain imaging studies that show that when there's different sets of information, we do pick up on it . . . We're just beginning to look at how people process those differences. We've got evidence that people will respond to a mismatch differently, because we're seeing different brain patterns for matches and mismatches" between words and gestures.

So our gestures sometimes convey different information from our words, and our unconscious minds take note of those differences and process them. If you think about it from your personal awareness of the world, it makes perfect sense. We've all had the experience of conversing with someone who says one thing but gestures another, and we get what they mean from the gesture.

Goldin-Meadow worked out a very elegant, simple test for this. She had subjects listen to a story that involved a stairway. The researchers made the gesture for a spiral staircase, but didn't verbalize that idea. Yet when they tested the subjects, they got the spiral staircase idea.

In another study Goldin-Meadow conducted, children whose teachers produced "grouping" gestures while explaining an algebra problem were more likely to talk about that idea later, even though the teacher hadn't discussed it at all. Concepts introduced via gesture are picked up by the unconscious mind and can be vocalized later even if the speakers are not aware of the concepts consciously.

But Goldin-Meadow is honing in on a further aspect of gesture and speech, one that has fascinating implications for why we gesture. As she puts it, "If you gesture, it lightens your cognitive load." By that, she means that it takes less mental effort to speak while gesturing. She goes on, "We don't really know why that is. We just know that it is."

It's a mystery, but the implications are important. You need to gesture. If you don't, you're making your brain work much harder. So those power gestures you've been taught, where you in effect limit your natural gesturing to some spider-doing-pushups-in-a-mirror gesture because some coach told you that makes you look intimidating, actually make it harder for you to think on your feet—leading to a less intimidating you.

Goldin-Meadow sums it up: "Gesture isn't just a reflection of speech." One theory is that gesture predated speech in our evolution. We spoke with our gestures before we learned to vocalize. But whether that's true or not, those gestures are important to our thought processes, to helping us communicate.

Let's Go to Harvard

I've observed this phenomenon at work in a small-scale experiment I ran on some Harvard midcareer Fellows a couple of years ago. We had a group of about seventy of (very) high achievers. I wanted to see the effect of gesture on how they presented themselves to each other.

The experiment was very simple. I asked them to introduce themselves to each other. So, one by one, the Fellows stood up and took a minute or two to speak about themselves. I gave them no guidance beyond asking them to "introduce themselves."

Then, after each one had finished, I took the speaker aside and asked him or her to adopt a specific gesture and then give *exactly the same introduction again*. I was curious to see the effect of open gestures on the thought processes and verbal patterns of people speaking in front of groups like these. The gestures I asked them to adopt varied, but mostly consisted of some form of open arms, exposing the torso to the audience.

Most of the speakers, before I coached them the second time around, in fact clutched their hands nervously in front of their stomachs, behind their backs, or at their sides. So the effects of my instructions to them were to greatly increase their openness to the audience.

The results were astonishing. In every case, the amount of personal information the speaker divulged greatly increased on the second try, when he or she was forced to be open through the open gestures.

I'll never forget one student in particular, who, on his first introduction, stated his name, in a flat, unemotional way, and then proceeded to identify his year in the program, the courses he was taking, and how much longer he had to go.

Then I coached him to open his arms out at his sides like a preacher at an altar, what I call the "Jesus gesture," with the palms upturned, just a little above waist high, and about twelve inches out from his sides. Try it yourself. Stand up and adopt the posture. Then imagine yourself talking to a group of seventy people, holding that gesture, for two minutes.

The student's second introduction was extraordinary and transformational. He said, "I've just come back from spending two years in Iraq, working with children. I saw atrocities committed that should never be done to anyone, let alone children, and I've made it my life's work to try to improve the lot of children around the world. Please join me in working to save children from the terrible mistakes adults make in war zones and other trouble areas worldwide." That was the gist of it; his speech was more impassioned and eloquent than that.

The audience rose to its feet and spontaneously gave him a standing ovation. A number of people came up to him afterward and asked how they could help. When I asked those in the audience to describe the difference between the two introductions, they spoke passionately about the second introduction and how it had moved them. The first one had failed to move them at all. When I asked them if they had noticed the Jesus gesture, none had!

Recall that I had instructed the speaker to give the same introduction. When I debriefed the speaker, he remarked that the first time he had been nervous and hadn't said much. But the second time, he felt inspired to share his heart with the audience more directly.

It was an extraordinary demonstration of the power of gesture and how we present ourselves to others to affect our interpersonal communications.

Gestures Determine Thought—and How Other People Take You

We're "read" unconsciously by the people around us. We convey our attitudes through our nonverbal signals much more powerfully (and directly to the unconscious) than we do through our speech. So when we try to get a sense of our personal presence—how we're showing up—we need to understand that our physical actions and presence are what convey our persons or our personality to others. It's all the more powerful because it's unconscious.[11]

As Goldin-Meadow has found, important information is communicated unconsciously through gesture even in normal conversations. Listeners tested afterward don't know which information comes from gesture versus speech. Some studies show that if a listener copies the gesture a speaker makes, the listener is more likely to like the person and attend to what he or she said.[12] I'll talk more about that phenomenon in chapter 2.

Goldin-Meadow says, "Gesture is a powerful tool. It can be used for good, or it can be used for evil." She's found that you can implant ideas in people's heads through gestures. They won't be aware that you've done so, but later on, they'll start to talk spontaneously about the ideas you've gestured about earlier. I'll talk more about that aspect of the power of nonverbal communications in chapter 6.

You think consciously about someone else's signals only when they're really strange or alarming or the person is really important to you and you're actively wondering what his or her state of mind is. But that unconscious activity determines an extraordinary amount of the effect you have on other people, the relationships you have with them, and your influence upon them.

As a first step, then, it's essential to get a handle on these unconscious cues.

Power Cue 1: How do you show up
when you walk into a room?

Body language is crucial to today's leaders because it tells us what we think about other people. People decode emotions primarily through gesture (and tone of voice). The emotional component represents a separate, nonverbal conversation that goes on parallel to the verbal one and typically a split second before the verbal one.

So leaders must master both conversations, but especially the second.

That conversation will make or break you as a communicator. Again, you may be entirely unaware of it, but it may confirm you as the top dog, sabotage your authority, connect you with your mate for life, get you in a fist fight (or out of one), win you a game or lose one, blow your chances at getting a raise, get you the big sale, lose you the prize or win it—and so on and on through most of the big moments in life.

How can you become more aware of this conversation that your body is having with the other bodies around you? Is it worth the effort? Will you become self-conscious and inauthentic if you do? Can you monitor what everyone else is "saying"? Is that helpful? Will it get you to places you won't otherwise reach?

Understanding the second conversation is key to leadership, because it's not something that you can leave to chance or the unconscious. There are simply too many decisions to be made, too many inputs to weigh, too many players to manage and lead. In the twenty-first century, the pace of leadership has accelerated, the flow of information has exploded, and the sheer physical and intellectual demands on leaders have intensified. You can't rely on common sense or instinct or winging it as you once might have done.

The first step to mastering your personal communications, then, is to figure out what you're saying in this second conversation. You'll need to take inventory of how you inhabit space, how you stand, how you sit, how you move, and how you interact with others. When you're sitting alone, do you slouch or sit straight? When you stand, are you taking up all of your space, or do you shrink into corners? When you move, do you move confidently or do you slink—or do you career?

What do your interactions with others look like? Do you come alive when other people are in the room with you, or do you go on the defensive?

In the next chapter, you'll learn ways to control those gestures. In this first step, you're just learning about how people naturally present themselves through posture, gesture, and motion.

As you work further on emotion, gesture, and your presence in chapter 2, you'll delve into the connection between these aspects of communications. But for now, I just want you to get a sense of your gesturing style, frequency, and intensity as part of the complete self-inventory.

When you have a moment, fill out the questionnaire at the end of this chapter to help you begin the process of gestural self-awareness.

Keep a Body Language Diary: Try to Catch Yourself Being Yourself

Try to catch yourself in unconscious behavior. You need to know how you're behaving when you think no one's watching—especially you. Try not to judge yourself. Choice and change can come later. For now, just be compassionate and nonjudgmental, and try to get a picture of how you inhabit space.

Your body is the physical embodiment of your unconscious attitudes, intents, and desires. As the old saying goes, in your youth, you have the face—and body—you're born with; by the time you're middle-aged, you have the face—and body—you deserve. So take the sting out of that saying and simply observe yourself and learn what those observations tell you about your attitudes, intents, and desires.

Be nonjudgmental. Just notice what you do.

If you have a hard time catching yourself unawares, then think about setting up a video camera when you're in a meeting or undertaking some routine chores. At first, you'll be self-conscious, and your behavior will be distorted from your usual mode of being, but after a few minutes you'll forget the camera is there. So be patient and use the video for what it can tell you about your habitual behavior, beginning a few minutes in.

As you watch, ask yourself, how am I showing up? Expressive or bottled up? Happy or sad? Active or passive? Strong or weak? What kind of person do I look like—to me? Someone who would be fun to meet? Someone imposing, or a wallflower? A nerd or a leader? And so on.

Keep a daily diary of your physical presence and emotional attitudes. Try to stick to this faithfully for about a week. Stop yourself once an hour or so and simply note what you're doing physically—sitting straight, slouching, fidgeting, smiling, frowning, and so on. Try to be as objective and nonjudgmental as you can. The process might take a few weeks, depending on how easy or difficult it is for you.

How do your gestures show up? Do you gesture a lot? A little? Are your gestures strong or weak? Are they expressive and fluid, or rigid and limited?

If you can take personal inventory in even a moderately detached way, you can take the first step to understanding yourself as an active presence in the world and decide what you want to do about it.

If you're having trouble being objective about yourself, then ask trusted (and supportive) family and friends to help. Ask them to rate you on a scale of one to ten for basic confidence, mood, charisma, leadership—how you show up. It's better to ask them specific questions like, "On a scale of one to ten, how normally cheerful would you say I am?" If you ask them, "How do I show up?" they probably won't have a helpful answer, because they're not used to thinking consciously in this way.

Ask your friends and family, but don't take too much stock in particular answers. Look instead for patterns. It's very hard for us to be objective about our closest friends and family, so don't expect too much. If you get a consistent pattern of comments across a number of people, then those observations are more likely to be accurate.

If you're lucky enough to be a rising executive in a company that regularly conducts 360-degree evaluations, they may be extremely helpful in this regard. Once again, don't put a lot of stock in particular comments; rather, look for patterns of comments about your usual mood, attitudes, or mode of being toward employees or colleagues. Remember, people are very good at unconsciously reading the emotional attitudes of people they know well daily.[13] We recognize when Bob comes in for work in a lousy mood, or Jane is excited about something. So look for patterns where people say that you're tough on colleagues, strong with employees, warm toward everyone, or the like. Those repeated patterns of estimations of your attitudes will tell you a lot about your physical presence, because it's from that physical presence that people figure out your attitudes.

How Big Are Your Butterflies?

Once you've completed this first step, becoming more aware of how you inhabit space nonjudgmentally, then it's time to begin to analyze your own body language more closely and definitively. Try it this way first. Ask yourself, *am I a confident person?* Note how many times you've rated yourself as nervous or self-conscious in your diary: any time you're behaving less than optimally because the pressure is on you in some way or you feel like you're performing.

Performance anxiety is probably the most common social fear that humans have. But people experience widely different degrees of this anxiety, and it's good to get a sense of where you are along the spectrum of normal behavior. Do you get nervous for most meetings or only the ones where something important is at stake? Do you get butterflies when you have to present to a team of six people or fewer, or only when you're presenting to a hundred people or more? Do you get nervous just for the first few minutes of your presentation or does your heart hammer for the whole session?

It's common to begin a presentation with butterflies in your stomach. Most people settle down after a few minutes; if you stay nervous for all or most of your talk, then you've got above-average anxiety. Similarly, if you get nervous even for routine meetings with small groups, then you've got above-average anxiety. It's normal to experience some nervousness for high-stakes meetings and large, special gatherings, but you're at the high end of the anxiety range if you get nerves when the stakes are lower and the numbers modest.

How Well Do You Understand the Second Conversation?

Once you've determined where you are on the confidence spectrum, then analyze yourself for your level of intuition. Do you generally know what other people are thinking, or do they regularly surprise you? Do you easily read other people's moods, or do you have trouble doing so? Do you notice a difference in the ease with which you read people in your intimate circles—family, close friends, coworkers you've known well for a long time—and people you know less well?

It's normal for us to be able to read people we know intimately, but not less close acquaintances. If even those in your closest circles of family, friends, and coworkers are often a mystery to you, then you have below-average intuition.

Men tend to be less intuitive than women, but on the whole most of us are not very intuitive, especially with people we haven't known very long. That gives those who are an edge over the rest; one of the purposes of this book is to show you how to increase the strength and precision of your intuition. I'll cover that in more detail in chapter 3.

When You Talk, Do People Listen?

Once you've estimated your intuitive abilities, then it's time to get a rough sense of your charisma quotient. The danger of self-deception here is very real, but do the best you can. Look at your diary and notice yourself when you're with others. How often are you the center of attention? When you speak, like the E. F. Hutton TV advertisement from the 1970s had it, does everyone listen, or not so much?[14] How often do you dominate a meeting, without much apparent effort, just feeling in the zone as you put your ideas across?

Do people hear you out, or do they stop listening before you're done? Here, it may be useful to imagine a range, where ten is some guru whose disciples hang on his every word, and one is a crazy homeless person in the street whom few people actually listen to. How do you rate yourself?

How about your own emotions? Are they close to the surface and easily accessed, or are you slow to ignite? Do your emotions mostly leave you alone, or are they constantly nagging at you, demanding your attention and reaction?

Most of us are not actually the center of attention most of the time. Those of us who do command attention more than occasionally belong to that select group of people the rest of us think of as charismatic. Most of us have charismatic moments, but those special few are "on" virtually whenever there's a group around them—and that's most of their waking hours. Most of us keep our emotions in check most of the time.

You may not have realized that there's a connection between those two sets of behaviors; there is. You can learn how to turn on charisma. It's controllable; it's not magic or something given to a select few at birth. Charisma is focused emotion, but I'll talk much more about that later. Showing you how to control your own charisma, so that you can turn it on and off when you want to, is another one of the purposes of this book.

Confidence, intuition, and charisma. These are the raw ingredients of mastery. Oh, yes, and one more: leadership. What kind of natural leader are you? Again, just try to note your behavior without judgment in these first few weeks on the road to mastery. You need to have a realistic sense of who you are and how far you have to go in order to get the most out of this book. So study yourself and your behavior when you're with your colleagues, family, and friends. When you make suggestions, do people generally go along with you? Do your plans, ideas, and feelings generally get implemented, acted on, and acknowledged, or do you feel ignored and misunderstood?

Natural leaders, by definition, are few and far between. Most of us are listened to occasionally; natural leaders effortlessly dominate the meeting, the occasion, or the party most of the time. Again, this dominance is something you can learn to switch on, augment, and create in yourself so that you can lead when you want to and follow when that suits you, too.

For now, you've completed your personal inventory, and you understand the connections among a complex of communications tenets: how you show up, how you create and transmit thought via your gestures, and how other people read you. You're ready for chapter 2.

The How-You-Show-Up Questionnaire

In each chapter, I'll include some notes on how to apply the ideas you've just learned. Let's start with a quiz about you.

Answer each question true or false, and give yourself 1 point for each true answer and 0 points for each false answer.

1. I am aware of how I am seated during the course of a business meeting.

2. I am conscious of what I do with my hands when I get into a spirited discussion.

3. When I'm interviewing people, I focus on their body language as much as on what they say.

4. I can tell when someone is bluffing.

5. I can tell when someone is lying to me.

6. I know, in a meeting with my boss, when she has decided to end the meeting before she says anything about it.

7. When I'm negotiating, I pay more attention to the opposite party's body language than I do their counteroffers.

8. I can tell when my coworkers are displeased before they say anything.

9. I usually get my way in team meetings.

10. When I speak, I have no trouble getting everyone else to listen to me.

11. I often know what people are going to say before they say it.

12. My voice carries easily so that everyone can hear me, even in a room with fifty people.

13. My intuition is strong; I often am able to read others without thinking about it.

14. When I walk into a meeting, I have no trouble sensing the mood of the people already there.

15. I can easily establish rapport with new people I meet.

Score

1–5 You need to increase your body language awareness.

6–10 You have average body language awareness.

11–15 You are ready for the World Series of Poker! You have above-average body language awareness.

CHAPTER SUMMARY

- For a long time, we've misunderstood the importance of gesture in our lives and communications.

- Researchers thought that the gestures that accompany speech were meaningless; now we know that they are meaningful and that they precede speech by a nanosecond or two.

- Researchers have studied how children learn, for example, and have determined that they learn nonverbally first.

- The first step in mastering your communications and leading the people around you is to determine what your own posture, personal presence, and gestures are like.

- Keep a diary or take video of yourself to determine—as objectively as possible—how you're appearing to others.

- Your self-assessment of your own confidence, intuition, and charisma will help get you started on the road to mastering leadership communication.

CHAPTER TWO

Taking Charge of Your Nonverbal Communication

Projecting Your Desired Persona— through Your Emotions

In this chapter, I will talk about how to gain mastery over your body language—your gestural vocabulary—by controlling your emotions. And I will discuss why that self-mastery is so important: because of mirror neurons. We all have mirror neurons in our brains that reflect the emotions of those around us. Emotions are contagious, and that has important implications for leaders.

The Difficulty of Paying Attention to Everything

So you've successfully taken a personal inventory of your own characteristic body language and developed a sense of how you look to others. That means that you've completed power cue number one and you're ready for number two. The good news is that, in some ways, the second cue is easier than the first—at least many people will find it so.

If you spent a few weeks getting to know your own body language, as I recommended in the first chapter, then you probably realized how much brain wattage it takes just to notice *consciously* something that's normally handled by your *unconscious* mind. The moment you started noticing yourself and your actions, you probably lost the flow of the conversation, became less aware of what was going on around you, or bumped into the furniture.

Power Cue 2: What emotions do you convey through your body language for important moments, conversations, meetings, and presentations?

We normally don't think at all—at least, in the casual sense of the word *think*—about where we are in space, how we're gesturing, or what kind of impression we're making on the people around us. Most of that activity is left to our unconscious minds most of the time. So when we do think consciously about such things, it's very distracting. Precisely because these chores are normally left to our unconscious minds, when we make them conscious, they tend to drive out other thoughts.

It's virtually impossible to monitor where you are in space, keep track of all your hand gestures, focus on the people around you, and keep up a steady flow of witty and to-the-point conversation, all at the same time. We may think consciously about body language on rare occasions, noticing when someone touches us or suddenly moves very close to us, but that kind of awareness is intermittent and brief and created by unusual body language, rather than the ordinary stuff. Constant self-monitoring is simply too difficult for most of us to manage. As the neuroscientists say, it takes too much cognitive load.[1]

But is it necessary? Why can't we leave that monitoring to the unconscious where it usually resides? Unfortunately, the answer is that we do have to develop some way of consciously creating the right kinds of body language in ourselves, especially in moments of great importance, because leaving it to chance won't work. We're far too likely to make two critical mistakes if we leave things to the gods.

Here's How You'll Go Wrong

First mistake? You'll project your nervousness and fail to command at the key moments of opportunity. Say you're heading into a key meeting, one on one, with your boss. The topic is your salary and, particularly, whether or not it should be raised. Let's say, not to beat around the financial bush, you need the money. You've moved to a new town when you took the new job, and the expenses of the new burg are proving to be higher than you expected.

There's a lot riding on the meeting, in short, so you're nervous. If you just leave your body language to chance, then you're going to convey your nervousness to your boss. Unless she's completely clueless and lacking in negotiation skills, she'll register that nervousness, read it as weakness or perhaps that you don't think you deserve the raise, and act accordingly. You'll be far less likely to get the money you were hoping for.

The second mistake you're likely to make, if you leave your body language to chance, is that you'll just convey a typical person's typically distracted state of mind. When you let your mind wander on an ordinary day, you might think about your to-do list, picking up milk on the way home, the TV show you saw last night, how sleepy you are, how you're not making any progress on your New Year's resolution to lose fifteen pounds, how annoying your office mate's voice is—all in the space of a few seconds.

If you walk into your boss's office thinking about all of that, your body language will reflect that mental list and it will be as diffuse as your mind. You will not be charismatic, powerful, or focused. Once again, your chances of getting the raise will be small to nil.

But if it's too hard to monitor body language consciously, and it doesn't work to let nature take its course, what's left? How do we solve this critical problem?

We need to find another way.

The Method behind Method Acting

Fortunately, the acting world stumbled on the solution at the turn of the past century in the form of Constantin Stanislavski. The Russian actor and director developed an approach to acting that involved identifying with the emotions of the character in the play so that the actor would feel the same things as the character and thus embody that character.[2] The goal was to bring the character to life in a way that seemed real, far more real than the highly stylized acting of the day.

To accomplish this feat, the actor strove to experience the called-for emotions by using sense memory exercises, conscious memories of a time when the actor had naturally felt that emotion. At the same time, Stanislavski urged the actor playing, say, a deckhand, to observe the mannerisms of real deckhands and copy those. The actor would work both from the inside out, from the emotion to the gestures that naturally followed as expressions of the emotion, and the outside in, from the typical gestures of someone in the situation the actor was trying to bring to life.

Now, it's important to understand that, in effect, real life was suspended for these actors, thus limiting what they had to achieve in the way of concerted gesturing. They had many weeks to prepare a play, and that play would have a limited number of scenes and emotions demanded of the actor. So the actor didn't have to learn how to behave spontaneously, but rather in certain limited, specific ways—ways that would be repeated night after night.

Your job is at once more difficult, because you typically don't get many weeks to prepare a scene where you want to show up powerfully in a certain way, and easier, because you're playing yourself. Just yourself in a particular mood.

How to Ace That Salary Review

Let's go back to the meeting with your boss. You want to make the case that you deserve the raise. You want to impress your boss with how worthy you are. You want to walk in exuding confidence and radiating control and power. In short, you want to walk in with the air of a winner—*someone who has already got the raise.*

So instead of trying to program every single gesture you'll use in the next thirty minutes or leaving all that to chance in order to focus on your verbal arguments (which is what most people do most of the time), you're going to spend a few minutes beforehand recalling a time when you felt like a winner. Pick a strong memory, a time when you won an award, let's say, came in first across the finish line, or perhaps simply were praised before all the other kids in class. Pick any memory that strongly evokes the right emotion in you.

Then use all the five senses—sight, smell, touch, hearing, and taste—to put yourself back in that scene. What did it look, sound, smell, feel, and taste like? Especially focus on sights and smells, because those will evoke the strongest memories and emotions for most people, but use all five senses as best you can.

For some people, this is an easy, natural exercise. For others, it feels weird and uncomfortable. But even if you're in the latter camp, practicing the exercise will make it come easier with time. With practice and time, you'll be able to think "confidence" or "I'm a winner" or whatever code words describe the emotion and moment for you and quickly focus yourself on that feeling.

Once you're able to do that, the rest will come easily. If you let your body feel the emotion through all the senses, you'll soon find yourself standing, gesturing, and acting like the winner you were and will be now. You'll stand straighter, pull in your stomach, breathe deeply, smile, pull your shoulders back—you'll do everything, in short, that telegraphs to other people that you're a winner. But you won't have to think about specific gestures, just invoking the feeling. Your unconscious mind will take care of the rest, because that's how you naturally express your emotions. That's the normal sequence of your brain: emotion leading to gesture and body language leading to conscious thought.

Indeed, the research shows that if you simply adopt the pose of a strong, confident person, your body will respond by making more of the right kind of hormones, the hormones consistent with good kinds of excitement and stress, and less of the negative ones. So working up a whole regimen of sense memory will create an even more powerful state and focus.[3]

Don't Focus Solely on Your Body

I don't recommend merely relying on adopting a confident physical pose without the mental work. The reason is, as I've described, as soon as you start thinking about other things, like the interview itself, you'll lose track of your posture and forget to stand like a winner. Very quickly your posture will revert to whatever it was previously, because it doesn't have the emotion to back it up. Controlling your own mind—your own emotions—is an essential part of projecting charisma.

A few more good things—happy by-products, in this sense—will happen as a result of this exercise, which you should get in the habit of performing before you undertake any kind of conversation, meeting, or presentation where the stakes are sufficiently high. Does it seem like too much work? It shouldn't. It's what successful athletes and performers do routinely every day for important races, meets, shows, and so on.

The first good by-product of this pregame activity is that you will become more charismatic. There's a lot of mystery and nonsense surrounding charisma. It's popularly supposed to be something that certain lucky individuals are born with—just a few great actors and politicians—or perhaps learn at some secret Charisma Camp somewhere that the rest of us are not privy to. But charisma is quite simple. It's focused emotion.

You know this in your own private life. Let's say you get some news, either very good or very bad, at work, and you go home brimming with it to your significant other. He or she is waiting in the kitchen for you and as soon as you see each other, he or she asks, "What happened?"

The question comes because you are focused, naturally, on the news and its emotional impact. The power of the particular feeling has driven out virtually every other thought. The result is that you're simply exuding excitement or devastation. For a rare hour or two, you have clarity of emotion and focus of thought.

How to Develop Everyday Charisma

That focused emotion is charismatic, and everyone around you will pick it up. We probably evolved to be able to do this because it was important to pick up quickly on strong emotions—like danger—in our early tribes. We can imagine life depending on everyone fleeing instantly when one of our gang came into sight full of the news that a rival band was on the other side of the hill, bent on destruction.

Now, beyond the cave, when we say someone is charismatic, that's what we mean. We mean that they're focused in some sense. Anyone who has met a charismatic politician will tell you that "she focused entirely on me for the whole thirty seconds!" or words to that effect. So whether the focus is on us or on an emotion, focus is charismatic. We feel it because we're wired to respond to strong emotion and strong purpose. Strong emotion sweeps everything and everyone else before it in human situations. We get caught up in the moment when someone is selling us with true passion, enlisting us into a cause with passion, or merely coming on to us with passion.

That's the secret of charisma: focused emotion. That's how great actors turn it off and on at will. They've trained themselves to first feel an emotion and then to focus on it to the exclusion of just about everything else. The result is that you can't take your eyes off them. It's not magic, but it is a technique that takes practice and hard work to master.

Start with the sense memory of a strong emotion that you naturally felt at some key moment in your life. Work at putting yourself in that moment, using all five senses. As you practice this exercise, you will gradually become better and better at focusing, with more fluency and more speed. I'll explain more about what to do before and during key meetings in the field notes at the end of this chapter.

I'll never forget, from my student acting days, watching a well-known Broadway actor demonstrate his ability to conjure up tears in a few moments. He was leading a class in working with emotion, and we students were complaining that it was hard work. He simply turned his back to us for perhaps a minute, faced us again, and revealed the tears that were streaming down his cheeks. He told us—his abashed students—through his tears, not to make such a big fuss about it, but just do it.

He had a whole retinue of emotions available at a moment's recall. Think about that ability for a moment. Does it make that actor inauthentic? It certainly made him a force to be reckoned with, for a reason that I'll get to—one that I didn't understand in my student days. But did it make him inauthentic? Is the ability to conjure up emotion at a moment's notice real or fake?

Why Do We Find Emotion So Compelling?

We don't ask the question of why we find emotion so compelling about somebody who is able to speak eloquently about a range of subjects, do we? So why reserve the suspicion for those able to be emotionally quick and facile?

It's because most of us are less able to manage our emotions, precisely because they're normally managed by our unconscious minds. They feel like something beyond our control and beyond our ken. They just well up inside us, like tsunamis. They're natural; they're not something we control. We put actors on pedestals and make celebrities of them because they can do something—manage this flow of human emotion and focus it—that the rest of us can't.

We make celebrities of them because the experience of emotions is powerful. The power comes because of a surprising ability of the human mind. To understand what that is and why it's important, we need to discuss mirror neurons.

Giacomo Rizzolatti and his team of researchers were working on research into the functioning of the brain, using monkeys as test subjects, back in the nineties, when one of the researchers noticed something odd.[4] The monkeys were hooked up to machines that registered their brain activity. As a reward for the various things the humans were getting the monkeys to do, the monkeys received peanuts, a food they love. When you give a monkey a peanut, he grabs it, and the pleasure centers of his brain light up like Christmas.

One day, the researcher absentmindedly—or perhaps with malice aforethought—ate one of the peanuts himself rather than feeding it to the monkey. The researcher was astonished to see that the monkey's pleasure centers lit up, just as if the monkey had eaten the peanut himself.

What was going on? After lots more investigation, the team discovered that monkeys and humans both have *mirror neurons* that mimic both actions and emotions of the simians and people around them. Our sense of empathy with our fellow humans, then, is real; when we see someone experience joy or sorrow, we experience that emotion with them. It's not that we appreciate the emotion or understand it intellectually from a distance. We actually experience it. We are an empathetic species.

Mirror Neurons Make It All Possible

As Rizzolatti explains, "The instantaneous understanding of the emotions of others, rendered possible by the emotional mirror neuron system, is a necessary condition for the empathy which lies at the root of most of our more complex inter-individual relationships."[5] What Rizzolatti is saying is that most of human relations would not be possible without mirror neurons, because we wouldn't be able to understand our fellow humans. And understanding is a first step in most human interaction.

This was an extraordinary finding with huge implications for communications and, indeed, most human relationships, including how we lead others. Rizzolatti says, "The mirror neuron systems . . . provided us with a base from which to investigate the cerebral processes responsible for the vast range of behavior that characterizes our daily existence, and from which we weave the web of our social and inter-individual relations."[6]

What are some of the ways that the mirror neuron system matters for communications and leadership?

Before getting to that, I need to discuss decision making briefly. Most people think of decision making as something that Mr. Spock, the logical Vulcan on *Star Trek*, does very well, and the rest of us, we humans, do not do so well. He keeps the emotions out of it, our thinking goes, and so he more rationally weighs the pros and cons and comes up with an optimal decision.

But that's a distortion of the essence of decision making. At its heart, decision making involves emotions, because emotions give us the ability to weigh the relative import of all the factors involved. If we're trying to decide what kind of new car to buy, for example, emotions don't just color every aspect of the decision-making journey; they make it possible. Let's say you're the cliché, a man in his mid-forties looking at a little red sports car, and your wife wants an SUV. Emotion, to put it very simply—how much you care about your wife versus how deep into your midlife crisis you are—is what makes it possible to weigh the merits of those two very different desiderata.[7]

Most of life is like that. The decisions we make in real life involve weighing different amounts of attachment and importance. Do you take the new job, which will involve moving to a new area, where you don't know anyone? Your feelings for your friends and family where you're currently living will guide that decision.

Don't Have a Stroke

We think that this sort of constraint makes decisions difficult, but in fact it's the opposite. There's a famous case in the neuroscience literature of a man who suffered a stroke that disabled the part of his brain, the hippocampus, which has a big role in handling emotions. The result? To everyone's surprise, he could no longer decide on anything. Why? Because he had no basis for choice. No emotions tugging at him to say, *choose this one, because it reminds you of your mother's eyes.* Or, *choose that option, because it will make your boyfriend happy.*[8]

So emotions make decision making possible. Mirror neurons make it possible for us to understand other people's emotions. As Rizzolatti notes, that makes empathy possible.

But think about it. Without empathy, communications of virtually any kind become, if not impossible, at least far more difficult. People who suffer from autism experience something very like this. It's what I experienced for a few months when I was seventeen, as I described in the introduction.

If communication becomes possible thanks to mirror neurons, then leadership becomes possible too, because what is leadership without the ability to communicate with your followers? Mirror neurons also help us understand why we find someone who is charismatic so compelling. By focusing on an emotion, the charismatic person is allowing us to feel it too. When President Bill Clinton famously said, "I feel your pain," he was absolutely right; he did, and so did everyone else. We all feel the pain, the joy, the fear, and the excitement that other people feel, and the more so when it's powerful, focused, or both.[9]

Mirror neurons make it possible for us to understand and entertain another point of view or another person's pain. Without mirror neurons, negotiating successfully with other people would be difficult, if not impossible, because no one would be able to engage in sympathetically understanding another person's emotions—the source of human connection, agreement, disagreement, conflict, and the rest.

Take Charge of Your Emotions and You'll Be Able to Take Charge

Which leads me to the second good by-product of learning to focus your emotions: once you take charge of your own gestures with the right techniques, you'll be well on the way to controlling the emotions and reactions of the people around you, thanks once again to those mirror neurons. That means that, for the first time, we're able both to understand how and why we can deliberately induce emotions in other people in order to fire them up for a difficult task or share a strong feeling with them that enables them to work together with a group they had been suspicious of before, and to create trust quickly with a group by creating specific emotional responses in its members without them being consciously aware of the manipulation.

Most of us usually go through the day with a cacophony of emotions roiling through our heads and hearts. We're panicked getting ready to go to work. We're furious at the guy who just cut in front of us on the freeway. We're overwhelmed by the emails waiting for us when we get to the office. We're intimidated by the meeting with the boss, where we have to explain how far behind the project is.

These emotions are reactive and (usually) counterproductive. They're certainly useless for leadership. Instead, you need to gain mastery over your emotions by consciously focusing on one emotion at a time, so that both you and the people around you find your presence calming, inspiring, or motivational, every day.

Does this emotional control seem Machiavellian? You prepare the content of a speech, a meeting, a negotiation. You wouldn't go into an important meeting and just babble about everything that was on your mind—your to-do list, your relationship issues, your golf handicap, your unresolved problems with your mother. No, you plan your remarks, at least at some level. You don't say everything that you think. You make strategic verbal choices. Why not do the same with emotions?

Most of us don't radiate a lot of charisma because we're not authentically present, right there, in the moment, and because, as I've discussed, even if we are present, we're not expressing much in the way of emotion. Either we are split in focus, nervous, thinking about something else, distracted, or we're bottled up, afraid to show what we really feel.

How then do you increase your own charisma? *First, increase your authenticity.* That means being absolutely aligned in what you say and how you say it—content and body language. You can't be authentic if those two modes of expression are not aligned.

Second, increase your passion. Focus in yourself on how you feel about the moment, the people you're with, the situation you're in, and then express that.

Focusing on both these steps will create a virtuous cycle that will increase your charisma quotient as you get more and more practiced at expressing emotion authentically.

While consulting with an executive on body language, charisma, and presence, I noticed something odd about the way he was standing as we worked on a mock interview. I was playing a high-status person, because one of the issues the executive wanted to address was showing up well with his peers—other executives, similar-status colleagues, and so on. The executive was essentially freezing in place as soon as he started conversing with me. That reminded me of studies of conversations between different-status people. One finding is that when a lower-status person is talking with a "superior," he or she tends to freeze in place.

So I halted the role-play and asked the executive what he was thinking about. He reported that he was working very hard on thinking about what he was going to say next. Was it that the mental effort required was causing him to freeze up, or was it his feelings of lower status?

Either way, the unconscious effect on me was to elevate my status and to signal to me that this client was low on the totem pole. The important point is that it didn't matter what the executive was consciously thinking about; what mattered was the way he showed up. To anyone else in the room, he looked like a peon, not a player.

So we worked on loosening up this executive's body language and getting him to think like a Jedi master. As I've said, either you can work from the inside out, on your emotional intent, or you can work from the outside in, on freeing up your body to look and feel like a top dog.

Either way works; if you can do both at once, you'll get there even faster. What happens if you start with both is that you get a good feedback loop going; your mind says, "I'm a player! And yes, I must be a player because I'm standing like one." If you start with the mind, it signals to the body what to do. Your unconscious mind dominates your behavior, but you can inject a new idea into the unconscious mind either way. The results are well worth it. If you want to become a top dog, you have to first act like one.

Your New Premeeting Ritual

To focus your emotions in preparation for a big meeting, work on what actors call the "offstage beat."

What is the offstage beat and why do you need it as a businessperson? Actors divide their scripts up into beats, basically short sections of the script when they're feeling one emotion or have one thing they're trying to accomplish—an "objective" in actor-speak. So, in *Romeo and Juliet*, when Romeo has exchanged insults with Tybalt and starts dueling with him, the beat might be something like, "I'm angry at Tybalt and want to kill him (despite my promise to Juliet not to fight with members of her family)."

The *offstage* beat is the emotion and objective you go on stage with. The idea is that a character doesn't just spring into life when he or she starts uttering lines, but comes from somewhere, wanting something, doing something, and so on. When an actor comes on stage with something already going on, she is much more interesting to watch than if she's just making an entrance in order to start speaking. Look for it the next time you're in the theater. You'll be able to tell actors who come on with an offstage beat, and those (if there are any) who don't. The difference is huge.

So as a businessperson, you'll be much more interesting to your colleagues if you start with an offstage beat before an important meeting. While you're breathing before the meeting, get an objective and an emotion into your head. It might be something like, "I can't wait to tell these people about my special new idea and I'm thrilled to the max to see them."

The other advantage to this activity, besides making you a far more interesting person right out of the box, is that you will spend less time making yourself nervous, which is otherwise the offstage beat you will have. The difference is absolute. A person with an offstage beat comes into a room focused, ready, energetic, and interesting. A person without one comes in . . . nervous. Not a pretty sight.

Do you find it difficult to focus your emotions? Try modifying your gestures—working from the outside in. You've got a much wider range of expressive options that perhaps you realize. Most people hold their elbows close in to their sides protectively and wave their hands from the elbows on down. I call this the "penguin gesture," and it's not very expressive. It signals to everyone around you that you're nervous, feeling exposed, or shy.

When you use the penguin gesture a lot, it will restrict your gestures in other ways as well, because of the way the body signals mood and intention to the mind. So, you'll tend to stand or sit in one place and gesture less effectively with your face as well. In other words, the whole second conversation of body language shuts down. The result? You'll signal to the world that you're trapped and narrow-minded, and what's more you'll increasingly act that way.

Don't get trapped by limiting your hands to a tiny retinue of gestures. Gesture from the shoulder, using the whole arm. Talk with your hands, to the extent that you can do it tactfully and appropriately for who you are.

Keep your gestures open. Don't fold your hands in front of your chest or crotch or put them behind your back. All of these are defensive gestures and will not inspire trust with your colleagues. Keep your gestures open and reaching toward them.

Projecting Charisma in Front of a Crowd

It's one thing to focus your emotions for a meeting with a couple of colleagues, but for many of us, this feels almost impossible to do when we're speaking in public. I've written at length in two earlier books about how to get better at public speaking, but here's a brief primer in public speaking success and charisma.

Public speaking is hard to do, and very hard to do well, because it requires you to embrace something that you've evolved never to embrace: recklessly rejecting the urge for self-protection. Yet, that's what you have to do to become more charismatic and thus successful as a speaker.

The whole weight of the history of our species leads us to value self-protection. When you stand up to speak, in front of a crowd, if feels as if you're risking that.

Now, you are risking something. You can fail to engage the crowd, you can make a fool of yourself, or you can attempt too little or too much and miss the mark. While the risk is almost always greater in your own mind than in reality, it is a risk.

Naturally enough, that's what's on most people's minds at the moment they begin to speak. They're thinking to themselves, "Why did I agree to do this? It could all go horribly wrong! People are going to think I'm an idiot!" or something along those lines.

The result of that emotional self-talk is a series of behaviors that, alas, tend to increase the likelihood that precisely the feared result will occur. People who fear failure in speaking are defensive, and that defensiveness shows up in a variety of ways, all bad. They may pace nervously—the familiar "happy feet" of some speakers. They may clutch and unclutch their hands in front of their stomachs. They may cross their arms, hide their hands behind their backs, or keep their arms firmly fixed to their sides, only waving their forearms in the penguin gesture.

All of these gestures and others signal nervousness to the audience. But more than that, they signal that the speaker is trying to protect himself. The speaker, in fact, is shutting off part of herself from the audience.

As you've learned in this chapter, if you radiate nervousness to the audience, it will become infected with that nervousness. Thanks to mirror neurons, you'll reduce the entire room to a state of abject terror. Imagine how well that will support effective communication!

And there's the rub. The whole point of presentations, from the audience's point of view, is to see the speaker whole, to gain insight into this person who has the authority to stand up and speak to an assembly of fellow humans. If the audience senses that the person is holding back, its judgment is that the speaker is ultimately dishonest and so can't be trusted. That's not of course (usually) what the speaker intends, but that's the tough luck of public speaking.

If you're speaking, try to begin right away avoiding self-protection. Get over yourself and your nerves. Put your focus on the audience. Be *open* to the audience. If you can manage that, they will carry you and give you back far more energy than you put out. The irony is that the best way to protect yourself in public speaking is to give up any thought of self-protection at all.

Play the Top Dog to Be the Top Dog

If focusing your emotions and moderating your gestures is proving difficult for you, back up and return to the first power cue for a minute. Videotape yourself again and see if you've made any progress. See if you can tell the difference *physically* when you're more focused *mentally*.

Recently I was working with another executive who wanted to show up with more charisma. As the day progressed, we tried some role-playing of the situations in which the executive typically found himself. One was a one-on-one conversation with a potential client—a high-status client. The executive often became tongue-tied in these sorts of half-social, half-business situations and wanted some help in figuring out what to say.

I played the high-status client, and the executive played himself. The conversation was indeed a bit stilted, but as the role-playing continued, something else began to catch my eye. The body language of the executive was far more important to what was happening than his chitchat.

So we stopped the scene and showed him the replay. He was astounded. He said, "You look like a CEO; I look like an analyst!" In his lexicon, an "analyst" meant a lower-status person.

I had to agree. He looked like an analyst. How did he telegraph his lower status? His body language was partly closed; he was holding his hands defensively in front of his stomach. But more important was his posture: a slight slump in his shoulders, sagging inward and collapsing his chest. The executive was giving up all his authority by closing off and failing to take up the space that a CEO or high-status person must take. He simply wasn't taking charge, in physical terms.

He could see it immediately; that's the power of video. We talked through what he was seeing and what he could do to change it. In this situation, you change either your posture or your thinking. I always prefer working on both and begin with the emotional side of things, but some people get faster results from focusing on one or the other.

In the next role-play, the executive concentrated on feeling *and* standing like a CEO; the result was astonishing. He was transformed; his persona opened up with new authority and his chitchat even improved. The problem was not that he couldn't think of anything to say. The problem was that he hadn't figured out how to inhabit the role of a CEO. Once he saw what he was doing physically, he freed himself up to fill the role both emotionally and physically; the difference was immediate and profound.

Remember, every communication is two conversations, the spoken content and the body language. The body language always trumps the content when the two are in conflict. So in planning your content and failing to think much about your emotions, which drive your body language, you're leaving that to chance—the more important of the two conversations.

It's time to put the focus on the more important of those two conversations, the body language. To do that effectively, you've got to manage your emotions, because, as you've seen, it's too difficult for most people to consciously manage their body language. Step two in the journey to mastery of communications, then, is to begin to manage your emotions before important communications.

Remember Who's in Charge

If you're like most of us, you think about body language as follows: *I'm pretty much in charge of my body. I direct it, from the control tower in my head. I tell it what to do. "Make coffee," I say, and it goes through the motions. "Now drink it," I say, and it obliges. Sure, there are activities like breathing that I let it handle on its own, but that's mostly low-level stuff I don't think much about. In short, I live in my body, my brain rules it, and that's the deal.*

But actually, as we know now, it's much more complicated than that. In certain realms, like the realms of emotion, relationship, and personal safety, just to pick three, your body literally thinks faster than your conscious mind and rules the roost accordingly. In other words, the older, lower part of your brain, the one beneath the cerebral cortex, "thinks" nonverbally. And it thinks faster than your conscious cerebral cortex.[10]

So many of those things that you do, like hugging your spouse when you see him or her at the end of a long day, you do because you've had an emotional or physical thought first and a conscious *Nice to see you, honey* thought only afterward. The body is in charge, in some significant areas of human expression.

What I've found in working with many clients over the years is that whatever your body *does* under adrenaline in high-stakes situations, so your mind begins to *think*. So, for example (and this is important), if you're one of those people who tends to freeze under stress, the kind of person who sits in one position or stands in one place, speaks in a monotone, and gestures minimally if at all, then gradually your conscious thought will become more and more restricted as well.

You will experience the phenomenon I've seen again and again where the executive under stress becomes verbally limited, getting tied up in word knots and using the same few words over and over. Or you'll miss an obvious answer to a question or forget to make an important point.

The body rules, especially under adrenaline. It's just trying to keep you alive, so pay attention to it. What can you do about this phenomenon? If you find yourself getting stuck in some way, climb out of the rut. Force yourself to move, to change the subject. Take a short break, walk to the back of the room, or ask everyone to stretch with you. Anything that's not illegal, immoral, or fattening and that gets you doing something different. You'll find that your conscious mind and your verbal facility will come to life once again when you do.

FIELD NOTES

Charisma and the Body

Let's walk through a couple of key moments and talk about some common challenges you may face as you work on putting this power cue into practice.

Right Before an Important Meeting: Focus on Your Breath

What are you doing in those last few moments before you go into a high-stakes meeting or negotiation? Most people are just getting nervous. Or more nervous. They're thinking about all the things that can go wrong and all the ways in which they might screw up. They're worrying about being judged by their colleagues—and found lacking. In other words, they're sabotaging themselves.

Is there a better way to spend those last few moments? There are a couple of things you should be doing rather than picturing disaster.

First, you should be taking a couple of big belly breaths. Deep breathing (as opposed to hyperventilating) will calm and ground you and, over time, with practice, will become a physical act you do that will tell you, "this is going to be a success."

How do you breathe in this way? Imagine your body is an eyedropper, with the bulb as your stomach. Inflate your stomach (expand it) as you breathe *in*. Then tense your diaphragmatic muscles (the ones over your stomach and under your rib cage—the ones you'd tense if someone punched you in the stomach) and hold the air in for a few seconds. Longer if you can. Then slowly let the air out, pushing your (tensed) stomach in as you do.

Don't move your shoulders during this procedure; your shoulders should not be involved. When you're full of adrenaline and panicky, you'll tend to breathe from your upper chest, taking in shallow breaths, using your shoulders. The result is to increase your feelings of panic. You must breathe *deep* breaths, from the *belly*.

Those Taoist sages who live to be a hundred? They take a hundred deep, belly breaths per day, religiously. You might want to start the habit.

There's another reason to breathe, and it's a little more practical. It nurtures and strengthens the voice. I'll focus more on the voice in chapter 4. For now, just know that deep breathing will help make your voice stronger and more pleasing to the ear.

When You Walk into the Room: Communicate Power through Posture

You can win over or lose your colleagues in the first *thirty seconds* of meeting them with your body language and specifically your posture. Really.

How do you accomplish this feat—or avoid this disaster?

You've seen people who bound into the room with lots of energy and no doubt seen people who do the opposite—creep into the room with low energy and lots weighing them down. Which did you look forward to more?

So it's important to smile, move quickly (but not so quickly as to fall or injure yourself), and look as eager as you can. But there's more to it than that. The real secret lies in your posture. There are three ways to stand (and a fourth that's a combination of one and two), and only one of them is effective.

Think of how you look from the side, as if a straight line were being drawn through your head down to your toes. If you've got good posture, the one your mother used to tell you to have, then the balls of your feet, your pelvis, and your shoulders and head all will line up on that vertical slice.

Some people, however, project their heads forward. Most people who spend a lot of time at the computer do this; the computer work rounds their shoulders and pushes their heads forward. I call this the "head posture," sensibly enough. It signals subservience, humility, and deference to the people around you. Great for the Dalai Lama, who has a terrific head posture, but not so good for the rest of us who don't need (or want) to be as professionally humble.

Others project their pelvis forward. (Imagine yourself playing air guitar without the air guitar.) This posture, which is highly sexualized, is typical of teenagers and pop stars. Again, not so good for grownup businesspeople. You don't want your colleagues thinking of you primarily as a sex object. Really.

The third possible posture is the straight-up, lead-with-the-heart posture. Imagine a soldier, seen from the side, but relaxed across the shoulders rather than rigid. That's the heart posture, and it radiates trust, authority, and confidence—all the attributes you as a businessperson want to project.

(The fourth is a combination of head and pelvis, a kind of question mark. Most typical, again, of teenagers, who are both self-conscious *and* sexualized. Or intellectual rockers. Not good for businesspeople.)

So bound into the room and look happy. But more importantly, watch your posture. It will signal to your colleagues who you are, whether you intend it to or not.

During the Meeting: Occupy the Right Space

Once you've set the right tone with your posture, it's time to think about your body language in relation to the others. Let's talk about zones. Not getting in the zone. No, I mean the distances between people. We each have four zones of space that we maintain between us. The first zone is the public zone, and it's twelve feet or more. We tend not to take personally the stuff that happens in that zone; thus it's not very interesting to us. Between twelve feet and four feet is the social zone. That's more interesting and is the distance at which we make cocktail party chatter and check out potential dates and that sort of thing. Warmer than public space, but still cool.

From four feet to one-and-a-half feet is personal space. Here's where it gets interesting. As soon as you're in my personal space, I'm paying close attention. You might be dangerous, so I'll keep a close eye on you. You might even be friendly, in which case I can be more or less open, depending on how friendly I want to be in return.

From one-and-a-half feet to zero feet is intimate space. In this zone, we're both committed. For business meetings—any public occasion, really—don't go here. Both parties will feel very uncomfortable. It's why Americans and English travelers feel so awkward in Asia and some parts of the Mediterranean. Cultures there still have the four zones, but they're compressed. So someone else's personal space feels like my intimate space.

Back to meetings. Use the four zones wisely and you can greatly increase your zip as an executive. People today are information overloaded, and it's hard to get their attention. So you need to get in their personal space if you're really going to grab them (intellectually). Not their intimate space, their personal space. Then you and the other person will feel as if you're having a conversation, which is the norm for paying attention in our casual modern culture.

Use the four zones, but especially the personal one, for persuading your colleagues.

During the Meeting: Make Effective Eye Contact

Why would you imagine you could get away with *not* looking at your colleagues? That's just common sense. There's research that suggests that we tend to trust people who look at us and distrust people who don't because we think they're lying. And we're right. It is a sign of lying, though a not very reliable one.

But is there anything more to it than that? There are some important subtleties.

The first *sophisticated* rule of eye contact then is that if you're going to make eye contact, you have to do it with your eyes wide open. Not shut, or almost shut. If the lights are bright or you're nearsighted, that's tough. Learn to compensate. It's so basic to people's reading of you that you'd be better off wearing dark glasses if you're going to squint.

The second sophisticated rule of eye contact is that you actually have to make eye contact. With individuals. For up to thirty seconds. You can't look over the heads of the group, and you can't dart your eyes around nervously like a lizard's tongue. Imagine you're having a conversation with people—better yet have a conversation with individuals in the room—and look at them fixedly but not too fixedly, just as you would in a real conversation.

The third sophisticated rule of eye contact is that you should be monitoring the extent to which your colleagues are making eye contact with you. It's a simple way to gauge their interest in what you're saying. If 80 percent of them are focused on you, you're OK. If 80 percent (or even 40 percent) are focused elsewhere, you're in trouble.

Eye contact, like other aspects of human communication, can potentially convey many meanings. Make eye contact, to be sure, but be careful that you're doing it right.

CHAPTER SUMMARY

- It's hard to think consciously about your body language.

- To control your body language effectively, focus your emotions.

- Focused emotion greatly increases charisma.

- Mirror neurons make focused emotion even more powerful because you affect others; you leak your emotions to them.

- Emotions are the basis of decision making and, so, leadership.

- Prepare your emotions for important meetings, conversations, and presentations, just as you would your content.

_____

CHAPTER THREE

Reading the Unconscious Signals of Others

How to Recognize and Understand Emotional Cues in Gestures

This chapter will discuss the groundbreaking work of Paul Ekman, the researcher who discovered micro-expressions and sought to decode lying. It will offer a two-part method for reliably reading other people's unconscious body language and emotional signals—often before they're aware of them themselves.

The World's Greatest Expert on Lying Unburdens Himself

If Paul Ekman had met the Dalai Lama earlier, this book might have been a chapter shorter.

They met in 2000: the world's greatest expert on lying and the spiritual leader of millions. Ekman sat next to the Dalai Lama during a break in a multiday seminar in Dharamsala, India. The Dalai Lama took Ekman's hand and held it without saying anything for about eight minutes. In those moments, Ekman found himself changed forever.[1]

The seminar provided regular bio breaks for the participants, but the Dalai Lama took none himself and instead offered the forty-five-minute interludes for individual consultation. Ekman, a scientist and religious skeptic, was attending the seminar at the behest of his daughter, who had become interested in the Tibetan cause and was somewhat in awe of the Dalai Lama. Taking the opportunity provided by one of the breaks, Ekman was persuaded by his daughter to approach His Holiness.

Ekman tries to explain what changed in him: "I think that what I experienced was—a nonscientific term—'goodness' . . . I have no idea what it is or how it happens, but it is not in my imagination. Though we do not have the tools to understand it, that does not mean it does not exist." He says that he felt a kind of warmth emanating from the Dalai Lama—a psychological, not a physical, warmth. He goes on, "The change that occurred in me was very dramatic. When I left Dharamsala, I met my wife in New Delhi so that we could spend two weeks traveling in India. My wife said, 'You are not the man I married.'" He continues, "I now believe that this experience was involved in the end of my hatred; the platform for my too-ready anger was no longer in place, and so the anger itself receded."[2]

The Dalai Lama's charisma has helped him touch thousands of lives in this way and made him a powerful symbol of peace. But in a way it's lucky for us that he didn't heal Ekman any earlier than he did. Ekman's hatred—that emotion that so mysteriously vanished when the Dalai Lama took his hand and held it for about eight minutes—is important to us all because it had long provided the fuel for a career that led to an enormous advance in the understanding of human body language and deception. Not to mention Transportation Security Administration (TSA) policies that affect anyone who flies in the United States and indeed worldwide, and an American TV show, *Lie to Me*, that ran on Fox from 2009 to 2011. The show featured an Ekman-like consultant fighting crime and stopping terrorists with body language expertise. Ekman himself was a consultant to the show.

Ekman had grown up under the shadow of an abusive father prone to sudden, terrifying rages. That had given Ekman a powerful incentive to learn to read other people's body language in an effort to anticipate his father's fury and protect himself. As a result, Ekman devoted his professional career to the study of facial expressions, lying, and body language. He developed the Facial Action Coding System (FACS), now widely used to label and study human facial variation, that allows researchers to label precisely the entire variety of facial expressions. Along the way, he discovered something about our faces and emotions that no one had ever noticed before: micro-expressions.[3]

Your Micro-Expressions Reveal
Your Hidden Emotions

When humans have a strong emotion and try to conceal it, it's liable to leak out in very quick facial expressions that are contrary to the predominant facial expression the person is maintaining. For example, if someone is pretending that he or she likes another person, but actually despises that individual, a quick sneer will leak out for one-twentieth of a second and then be gone. The person is typically unaware of the leak, as are the people around him, except perhaps as a vague sense of discomfort or unease.

Ekman developed a training system that enables people to learn to spot these micro-expressions, and you can teach yourself to be quite accurate in detecting their presence and their specific emotional meaning.

Ekman has worked with the FBI and CIA extensively to train their officers in deception detection, and micro-expressions are of course an important part of that training. Ekman is quick to point out, however, that the ability to detect a micro-expression underneath a different, dominant expression doesn't necessarily tell you what the person is thinking or even what the expression means.

In other words, if you spot a flash of anger across the table during an important negotiation, does that tell you something about the other party's negotiating position? Not necessarily. It may only tell you that the negotiator is tired and the day has been long. Or that she just realized that she's going to miss her plane home.

Knowing the suppressed emotion doesn't necessarily tell you the meaning the person attaches to that emotion. And that's important. Ekman's work with the TSA, the FBI, and the CIA regularly bumps up against this problem. For instance, if you're watching a stream of people walking through a security line at the airport and one of them registers nervousness, is that person nervous because he's planning to blow up a plane, or nervous because he's afraid he might miss one and be late for his daughter's birthday party?

There are limits to what this kind of conscious training can tell you.

The further problem that Ekman and security people face every day is one that is much less important for you.

They're trying to read the emotional secrets of *strangers*, and a large number of strangers at that. Most of us deal only with a few people whom we know quite well and see over and over. There are some exceptions to that—as, for example, when you meet a new client or customer at work, or negotiate with someone new—but I'll deal with that issue later.

Use Your Unconscious Expertise the Way It Should Be Used

The good news is that you are already an unconscious expert, for the most part, in reading *some* of the body language cues and the concomitant underlying emotions of *most* of those familiar people. For example, arriving home, you can tell in an instant if your significant other is in a bad mood, right? Or at work, you know instinctively if your boss is in a really good mood for some reason or another. Or you can tell when a colleague is stressed out and unlikely to help you with something.

In other words, when one of your circle of friends, colleagues, and family is experiencing a strong mood, good or bad, you most likely can pick it up with relative ease. You pick it up unconsciously, and if the emotion is strong enough, it gets to the level of your conscious mind and you think, *He's in a good mood!* Or, *She's a bit tense tonight.* Then you may vary your tactics accordingly.

That's the good news. The bad news is that where you need the help is in the subtler moments when the emotion isn't so obvious, the stakes are very high, or that person you know well is making a surprising claim and you want to know whether or not she is lying. Or the person isn't part of your intimate circle; it's someone you know or have met professionally, and whose motivations and intents matter to you at certain specific times.

At those times, being able to accurately read other people's emotions can be extremely important and helpful for your work life or your life in general.

We need a system that will tell us more, however, than Ekman's micro-expressions, and without the complicated training. We need a system that will reliably help us out in a certain set of work and personal settings and situations. We need a system that will allow us to continue to participate in one of those situations, talking and listening, without having to take time out to study the body language in isolation. And we need a system that will have a high degree of reliability. You'll learn just such a system in this chapter, inspired by Ekman's insights, but more broadly applicable to work and home life—unless of course you work in the CIA. This method is one I've developed over many years of working with clients and reading other people's intentions through their body language. It's simple and effective.

The third step in the power cue process involves learning how to read the body language of others around you, accurately and easily, through questions you ask yourself.

Power Cue 3: What unconscious messages
are you receiving from others?

A couple of years ago, I flew down to an undisclosed location in the southeastern United States to train a group of Air Force Special Ops folks who were going to be deployed to a trouble spot in a Middle Eastern country. Their job was to parachute into the country, quickly establish relationships with the locals, and start building things. That, at least, was what they were willing to share with me.

Their question, sensibly enough, was how to ascertain the friendliness or hostility of the local people—fast. Lives depended on getting that right. So I taught them the two-step technique I'm going to share with you in this chapter.

First, I need to clear away some common misunderstandings about body language. There is a huge mass of misinformation that has built up around reading body language over the past half-century. The research approach widely followed since World War II studied gestures as if they had specific meaning. In other words, if you put your hand to your chin, you're thinking—in all circumstances—and so on.

Don't Be Fooled by Those Obvious Emblems

As I indicated in the introduction, research began with the specific gestures, like the peace sign and the upraised middle finger, that do have particular meanings, what the researchers called "emblems." Each culture may have only a handful of such gestures, but the approach then colored thinking about all the other gestures we make. Indeed, as discussed in chapter 2, the hand-waving gestures we make when we're talking were dismissed as meaningless and largely ignored.[4]

Now, researchers have made some headway. The problem with the previous approach is not that such a reading of a particular gesture isn't sometimes correct. The problem is that gestures are ambiguous, fluid, and multidetermined. So focusing on a particular gesture and insisting that it has a specific, singular meaning will get you into trouble. That hand on the chin may mean you're thinking, or it may mean you're tired and resting your head in your hands. Or it may mean you're scratching an itch surreptitiously and trying to look wise while doing so.

If focusing on particular gestures isn't reliable, what can you use to decode body language?

Your unconscious mind. It's already hard at work, practically 24/7, reading the body language of everyone who comes into your field of ken. What it looks for is intent. It checks people to see if they're powerful or subservient, friend or foe, on your team or somebody else's, and liable to tell the truth or lie— basic, simple intents like that. Intents that are very important for how you might interact with them.

For the most part, you're only vaguely aware consciously of all this unconscious mental activity. You typically only notice the really powerful emotions people bring into the room with them—fury, wild excitement, huge relief—in your conscious mind. Or, you may be more closely attuned to a wider variety of emotions from people you're particularly close to. As in Ekman's case, for example, if a parent is prone to sudden and alarming fits of rage, you may be on the lookout for that, so those warnings may leap to your conscious mind more easily.

Or again, if you're particularly interested in getting something out of another person—a favor, a deal, permission— then you may pay closer attention to his or her mood. In effect, you ask yourself, *what are my chances to get Jane to agree to moving that deadline?* Otherwise, you leave your awareness of other people's moods to your unconscious mind. Then, you'll most likely pick up a vague feeling about mood, or you may think to yourself after a conversation, *Henry seemed a little out of sorts.*

All That Unconscious Data Is Mostly That—Unconscious

Most of the time, then, your conscious awareness of your unconscious data gathering is limited and often comes after the fact. It has to be that way, actually, because the problem with the unconscious mind is that it gathers far too much information, rather than too little. It's noticing everything, and there's far too much data coming in, so you have to ignore the stream of information with your conscious mind or you'd rapidly be overwhelmed with mostly unimportant information.[5]

Think about all the tiny adjustments people make every second to the way they gesture, sit, stand, and walk. Each of those thousands of adjustments carries meaning about the intent of the people in question. *I'm tired of sitting here. I'm thirsty; where's that water? She's pretty. He's good-looking. What a bore! It's warm in here. I wonder when this is over.* And so on. Our physical bodies exist to carry out our intents, attitudes, and emotions. It's not that we don't get any information about other people. The problem is that we get too much. Your unconscious mind is constantly taking it all in, noticing that twitch, that stretch, that blink, and so on. Your conscious mind can't possibly keep up and still do all the things it has to do. And most of that data isn't terribly useful or interesting.

You're probably picking up Ekman's micro-expressions unconsciously, along with everything else. Because you haven't been trained, that information just adds to general impressions about other people you have developed and may think about consciously from time to time. *He's making me uneasy. I don't believe her. I don't trust him.*

How much more useful would it be if you could tap into that unconscious expertise when you wanted and needed to, in real time, to gauge the intents and attitudes of the people around you in specific ways? How much more useful would it be if you could anticipate their thoughts by realizing their decisions even before they were consciously aware of them themselves? How much more useful would it be if you could quickly ascertain important insights like *that person is lying to me?*

Let's Put Our Minds Together

What you're going to do is to strengthen the relationship between your conscious and unconscious minds in reading other people, so that you can read people swiftly and accurately. That's what the two-step process is for—ask yourself the specific question, listen for the answer. To do that, you're first going to establish some basic categories of clues to look for to begin to solve the problem of too much information. I'm going to give you clues to look for in each of those basic categories. Then, with that grounding, you're going to tune your unconscious mind to look for the answers to particular questions you have about people in real time.

All of this is going to take some initial work, and for the long term, it will mean some mental preparation before any key meeting or negotiation or conversation when you want to be attuned to body language. But once you get the hang of it, you'll find that your body-language expertise becomes quite strong and adaptable.

Let's get started. I'm not going to point you to specific meanings of specific gestures. Instead, you're going to think about four basic areas of interest and the *constellations of body language* that are indicative in each of the four areas. The idea here is to narrow down what you're looking for. That will train both your conscious and unconscious minds to begin to develop the expertise you need.

The four basic areas where it's commonly helpful to be body-language smart are: *power, friendship, alignment*, and *lying*. In terms of power, you often want to know, in both work and life, who's in power here? Who's the top dog, the decision maker, and who are the underlings? And who's in power at this moment?

For friendship, you are hardwired from caveperson days to want to know the answer to the question, *friend or foe?* for obvious reasons. Is this individual a threat? Does this cute person like me? Is this person someone I can count on, or is she betraying me behind my back? And so on.

With alignment, we're looking for signs of fundamental agreement or its absence. Is this person on my team? When she says she'll vote for me, does she mean it? Can I depend on Jim when the budget numbers start to shrink? Will he come through for me?

Finally, with lying, the reasons we care about this are once again obvious. We are all of us liars, every day, for the best of reasons. We tell her she looks great in that dress. We tell him he's still got what it takes. We say, *I really had a good time.* So we often want to know if someone is telling us the truth or not. Because we know that everyone is quite capable of lying, and as grownups, we learn to manage our faces reasonably well to disguise our contrary feelings when we say, *Thanks, that was great.* Beyond the social niceties, of course, the stakes are often much higher, and much—money, career, life choices—can hinge on knowing the truth or the lie.

Watch for That Telling Change

Before I dive into the four areas I'm going to focus on, let's go over a few general principles. For all body language reading, you want to first establish a baseline reading and then note differences. In other words, first check out the other person's or people's general orientation toward you and the others in the room and then notice whenever there's a significant change. That can indicate a change of heart, mood, decision, or simply a desire to discontinue the conversation. Think in terms of baseline and change. Keep it simple.

In this regard, remember to always consider the context. A person who suddenly closes down, for example, may not be indicating hostility, but rather thinks it's time to go. We often signal the end of a meeting with a change in body language that involves retreating, closing off, or disconnecting. That's not necessarily hostile; it just means it's time to go.

Overall, when we move closer to someone else, we're showing friendliness, trust, or connection. When we increase the distance, we show the opposite. Hand gestures tell a similar story. When people reach toward us with open gestures, they're usually signaling openness. Only rarely is it something else, like a left hook to the jaw. Reaching can indicate aggression, control, or an attempt to dominate. An embrace, the ultimate open gesture, after all, is a combination of open hand gestures and open torso, where we reduce the space between ourselves and someone else to zero.

Hands speak a constant language; learn to watch them for what they'll tell you. Are they placed placidly in the lap? Do they gesture elegantly and smoothly, or do they jerk and clench? Are they nervously kneading one another? Are the hands twitching constantly, or attempting to conceal themselves in pockets or behind the back? Hands are marvelous little weather vanes signaling the state of the soul within. You get regular updates from other people's hands about the state of their nerves, defensiveness, confidence, anger, happiness, sorrow, interest, or boredom, in addition to their openness or lack thereof. A recent study found that hands are a more reliable indicator of poker players' cards than their faces, which of course are proverbially poker-faced.

Finally, start to watch people's legs and feet. Most of the adults you'll meet are reasonably good at assuming bland expressions on their faces, but their legs and feet will likely tell a more revealing story. Look for overall orientation. Are those legs near you, pointed toward you, or not? Are those feet close to yours or pointing toward the door? Look for signs of discomfort or nervous energy, such as bouncing or fidgeting. That's a more reliable giveaway than that carefully neutral face.

How to Spot the Person in Power

Now let's dig into the four key areas of body language, starting with a look at powerful people and their body language.

Powerful people take up more space than other people. Their unconscious goal is control, so they control the room and the people by using more of it. They sprawl, splay, and extend their arms and legs. They take a bigger piece of the room, and they take bigger rooms—hotel rooms, for example. Tall people have a natural advantage in this way, because we unconsciously equate height with power. Our unconscious minds seem to like that sort of analogy. That's why tall people are statistically more likely to get paid more and rise higher in their professions than short people.[6] Of course, you can no doubt think of many short exceptions to that rule, but we're talking averages and the unconscious mind.

Powerful people talk differently than weaker people, interrupting more, taking more conversational time, and using longer pauses. They get to control the tempo of the exchange with other people, deciding whether to make more or less eye contact, employ more or less touch, and take more or less time.

Powerful people may withdraw temporarily from a conversation, leaving the rest of the conversation and the details to underlings, for example. In subtler ways, powerful people may show their ability to come and go by leaning back during a meeting and putting their hands behind their heads to show temporary withdrawal or superiority over everyone else. It's arrogant but effective. You will know when you are in the presence of someone who believes she is powerful because of the signals I've described as well as others, such as your own tendency to be obeisant in front of the person.

How do you assume authority when you want to manage it consciously? Stand as tall as you can, holding your head high and throwing your shoulders back. But keep your chin level; if you raise your chin, you'll look like a punk, or worse, like Don Corleone in *The Godfather*. Make sure you are the tallest person in the room if you can. Give yourself a taller chair if you're sitting. Fans of *The Daily Show* will know that the host, Jon Stewart, is quite short, and does his best to maximize his height by making his guests come to him. He's standing on a platform surrounding his desk, so the guests have to climb up to get to him; the visual the audience gets in this way maximizes Stewart's stature.

Finally, move less—in fact, as little as possible. Like Stewart, get everyone else to come to you if you can. Stay still and say less. Let other people come onto your turf.

Those, broadly speaking, are some of the ways that power plays out in body language in daily organizational life worldwide. That is one example of a meaningful cluster of body language signals that you can learn to decode with reasonable reliability.

Let's move on to the other three basic areas. Besides power, you want to know if people are truly friendly or faking it. You want to know if people are truly aligned with you or not. And you want to know if they're telling the truth or lying. Those are the basics.

How to Tell Who's Friend or Foe

Let's go next to that most fundamental question, *friend or foe?* Here, it's useful to start with the face, even though, as we've learned, part of being adult is to learn to manage your face with reasonable success. We're going to look for openness.

Open faces tend to have four particular characteristics, in contrast with faces that are more closed. First, open eyes are— open. Wide open. Narrowed eyes are the opposite indicator. If you're close enough, check out the pupils. Pupils dilate when we like what we see and they close down when we don't.[7]

Second, if we're feeling open, we often raise our eyebrows. When we do that, we're really asking the question, *what do you think?* Or, *what's your response?* I always look at people's foreheads once they've reached a certain age. If they have wrinkles, good. That means that they've been open and receptive a good deal in their lives up to that point. A smooth forehead sets off alarm bells in my mind because it suggests the opposite. That it doesn't tell me *why* that person has been habitually closed down. There may be very good reasons: growing up in an abusive household or a repressive country, for example.

Third, look for smiling and nodding—or their opposites. Most adults, of course, can control their smiles and nods with some conscious success, but if you look for a pattern over a couple of hours, you'll get a reasonable idea. You need to beware of gender, cultural, and status differences here; each of these can affect how much a person smiles or nods.

Now look at the rest of the body. Here's where the non-verbal fun really begins. Basically, friendliness means closeness. Friendly people get closer to you, they keep their torsos pointed toward you, and they don't block their torsos off with their arms or hands. The opposite of any of these large motions can indicate closed intent or outright hostility—moving away, blocking off the torso, or pointing it away from you.

How to Tell Who's Aligned with You

Third, let's consider alignment. By that I mean the age-old question, *is this person on my side or not?*

Back in the days when I was working in politics, I learned quickly that *whose side are you on?* was the main—and often the only—question that politicians cared about. Because politics is all about the trading of favors and influence, trust is enormously important to the players. They're always scanning the troops for signs of incipient betrayal, and the best ones rely enormously on their gut sense of whether or not the person in front of them is aligned with them or not.[8]

So you look for overall orientation. People who are in agreement with one another tend to mirror each other. One leads, the other follows in a matter of a few seconds. It's especially revealing and easy to spot when there are three people talking; typically two will align and mirror and the third will not. All of this makes for entertaining people watching. Once you're sensitized to this aspect of behavior, you'll find it's easy to spot.

When you're trying to get a read on who in the group is for you and who is against you, start by looking to see who has the same basic body orientation as you. To test agreement, move and see if the other person mirrors you in the next thirty seconds or less. Spouses, partners, and lovers usually mirror one another's physical orientation when they're together or with others and they're in basic agreement. It's interesting to watch couples for signs of mirroring—and its opposite. You can often detect trouble in the relationship before the couple is aware of it.

People who are profoundly sympathetic to one another—lovers, siblings who are close, even business partners—are fun to watch because they will move together virtually as one. When you see this kind of unconscious dance, it's a strong signal that the two people are in intimate agreement, either mentally or physically or both.

What happens in mirroring is more profound than just agreement or even connection, however. Because persuasion is an emotional as well as an intellectual activity, it comes from deep within the brain. When we are strongly aligned with someone, we do so with our whole bodies. You can use this to drive agreement and create persuasion. Adopt a posture, and watch for others to adopt it. Once they have, change it slightly. If the others go along, you're well on your way to persuading the room. I'll talk more about how to use unconscious signals of alignment in the field notes for this chapter.

For now, know that our minds say to ourselves, *I'm aligned physically with this person, so I must agree with her*; mirroring in fact builds agreement and is itself persuasive—unconsciously. It's the more powerful because it's unconscious.

The unconscious mind knows all about alignment. We learn early on, in the cradle, when we watch our parents (the ones who love and care for us) mimic our behavior, just as we learn to mimic theirs. Mother will tip her head so that it mirrors ours, and we'll coo madly at each other. That's where it all begins.

How to Tell Truth from Lie

We all want to know, at key moments, whether that person who's looking us in the eyes with apparent sincerity is telling the truth or not. *You can trust me. I wouldn't lie to you. I really mean it this time.* When you want to believe someone, it's even trickier, because people have a tendency to grasp at the signs of honesty and suppress the warning signals of fibbing.

Ekman says that we can't ever be sure whether someone is lying or telling the truth, but I don't agree. He's focusing on a different situation and a different standard, looking at strangers, enemy agents, the FBI, and so on. He's particularly concerned about pathological liars, who are expert at concealing the traditional signs of lying, because of course law enforcement officials have to deal with those monsters far more often than the rest of us.[9]

Beyond that, our situation is different in another way. We care about people who are mostly well-known to us. We know a great deal about their normal behavior much of the time, so we can determine with high reliability when they are lying. The good news is that the traditionally described clues for lying are reasonably accurate.

Start with the eyes. If you see the clichéd clues to lying—rapidly darting eyes, lack of eye contact—you've got a good likelihood of deception. Most of us deal with normal, decent people most of the time, and lying for them is an uncomfortable activity. None of us likes to do it, so we signal our moral discomfort with obvious physical discomfort.

But also look for the opposite taken to an unusual extreme. If you know the person well, look for an attempt to control the eyes (and the rest of behavior) with unnatural stillness. If you're suddenly getting wide-eyed, frozen innocence from a teen who hasn't looked you full in the face for weeks, then she's probably lying about where she went with the car last night.

Beyond the eyes, look at the way the person holds his or her head. When a person lies, he turns his head away or tips it up or down so as to move it away from the other person. We love to get out of intimate space when we lie, because most of us don't like to lie to our intimates. So watch for the eighteen-inch barrier. If someone close to you, an intimate, suddenly pulls out beyond the intimate-personal barrier of eighteen inches, then that may be a sign that he or she is lying. At the very least, something is making him or her uncomfortable. Let's hope it isn't simply what you had for lunch.

Look also for that overall sense of feeling, the most reliable way to tell that your unconscious is talking to you. Look to see if the torso is turned away or toward you. See if there are defensive gestures from the hands and arms and signs of agitation from the hands and fingers. Look for contradictory behavior from the legs and feet.

Finally, listen for signs of strain in the other person's voice. If your loved one carefully controls her voice or it comes out a little higher pitched than usual, she or he may be attempting to conceal something. Ekman has found that people who are lying slow down their speaking and even their facial gestures and other mannerisms. But ordinary people can also rush to get through an awkward-feeling moment. So the main thing to look for is different behavior from what you usually see. You'll soon pick it up if you pay close attention!

How to Tell If Someone's Listening to You

Real listening is not one of the four key questions, but it is important to predicting success in any meeting—and unfortunately, it is becoming a rare commodity. We're living through a disconnected era in our nanosecond-based, 24/7, ADD, mostly virtual world. Our colleagues and fellow workers nod and smile a lot to show that they're listening, but it's not really happening. Real connection is rare. Their internal monologues are too intense, too scared, and too focused on their own survival—*Will I still have my job? How can I pay my mortgage? Are my kids staying out of trouble?*—for us to compete in the attention stakes.

In short, we have an epidemic of fake listening. It's the kind of listening that really means the other parties are just thinking up what they're going to say next, if they're on the same conversational planet at all.

What are the body language signs of fake listening? The eye contact is too fixed and too still. A person holds his head very still, as if to show that he's really focused on you. Or she smiles too brightly, holding the smile too long. But a real conversation is full of anticipatory nods and handoffs of eye contact in order to allow smooth conversational ping-pong. It's relaxed and synchronized. Fake listening feels very different from that. It's tense rather than fluid, abrupt rather than smooth, hyped rather than natural.

And that's just the face. Watch the rest of the body. Is it turning away from you? Is he tapping his fingers? Is she pointing her feet toward the door? Is the other party in constant motion, never quite coming to rest during the conversation? These are all signs of connection deficit syndrome.

Don't do it. Take the time to connect with other people by being truly present. Let your own mind go quiet and instead of chattering away to yourself—or planning your escape—focus on the other person with the intent to connect.

You'll be amazed at what you can learn. When everyone else is moving at a hundred miles per hour, start your own slow connection movement.

How to Read a Handshake

Want to start the process of reading someone's body language from the moment you meet him or her? You can learn a good deal about someone by watching the other hand—the unshaken one. At the same time, if you don't want to commit a social solecism, you still have to shake hands properly. So it's a lot to do, sure, but it's not impossible.

Grab the person's hand, give it a firm squeeze (but not too firm), and look him or her in the eye. For about two or three seconds. Then, check out the other hand. A quick glance should suffice. Let's not make this too difficult. It's not.

What can you learn from the other hand? A surprising amount. It can be either closed or open, hidden or visible. Look for the more extreme forms of behavior for more significant clues. And remember that all body language is multidetermined, so it needs to be checked against other sources of information, other impressions, and subsequent messages given and taken.

An open hand is good; a clenched hand may be a warning sign of some tension or a hidden agenda. If the other hand is hidden, that may be a sign of concealment of some issue or feeling—or it may just indicate shyness. Again, you need to check any hints you get against other sources of information about the person.

The most neutral position—and the one you should adopt yourself if you want to show up in the best possible light—is open, relaxed, and at your side. If you want to be particularly welcoming, point your palm toward the other person, while keeping your hand open, relaxed, and at your side. Sound complicated? It's not; try it. It's surprisingly easy to make automatic.

The point is that your hands talk, as does your whole body, even while you're engaged in routine behavior like shaking someone's hand. Keep an eye out for telltale clues away from the shaking hand, and you'll be surprised at how often you learn something interesting.

Now That You're an Expert, Your Education Really Begins

That's a crash course in reading other people's body language consciously, in terms of groupings of suggestive physical behaviors. Remember that you should always establish a baseline first, and that variation from the baseline is the most reliable indicator of a strong body language signal. Remember, too, to look for lots of evidence, not one gesture or even two. Finally, remember to look for the answers to one of the four basic questions, not just random body language in general. Ask yourself, for example, *what am I seeing, truth telling or lying?* You'll have a better chance to get a reliable answer.

That's the first step in learning to read other people's unconscious messages. But it's only the first step, and you're only armed with four basic questions. You need to go deeper than this if you're to arrive at a reliable way to read a broad range of body language in a wide range of situations with the possibilities of a near-infinite number of questions, without spending a lifetime studying it constellation by constellation, like body language astronomers with endless time and a universe of stars to study.

We Need to Involve Our Unconscious Abilities

How are we going to reach this higher level of body language awareness? We've begun to train our (conscious) minds in body language awareness through groupings of body language and basic questions of intent. Now, we need to focus less on the visual clues and more on the underlying intents. We need to use our conscious minds less and our unconscious minds more. We need to leave Ekman behind and develop a new way of harnessing his insights with greater applicability. We're not all CIA agents or moles, and we don't have their specialized training. We need to start harnessing our *unconscious emotional expertise* to tell us what we want to know.

That's going to take a little more training.

Here's how it works. Think about gestures as an early warning system for mood. We gesture because our unconscious minds push us to do so with an emotion, an intent, or a desire that our conscious minds are unaware of until after the gesture has started. Our bodies know what we want before our conscious minds do.

That means that any given gesture is a physical embodiment of an intent. We just have to ask ourselves what that intent is. The body in question already knows. Our bodies most likely already know, because they've performed similar gestures in similar circumstances. The unconscious mind knows; it directed the gesture. It's just a matter of bringing all that knowledge up to the conscious mind.

So bring the power of your unconscious mind to bear on the problem. Get it to speak to you. Learn to listen to your unconscious mind. It is there, all the time, keeping you alive and monitoring your surroundings and the people around you for threats and opportunities. It's telling you that you're hungry, angry, bored, or happy and content. It's running your life for you, and you're largely unaware of its existence, except in unusual moments when your gut speaks powerfully to you—*I don't trust that person!*—or you duck when a shoe is thrown at you.

How to Use Your Intuition

If you've ever had the experience of déjà vu or a sudden, strong intuition about a person or something that was going to happen, then you've heard your unconscious mind trying hard to get in touch with you. If you've ever had a gnawing sensation in your gut that things just aren't going right, despite the fact that on the surface, the day seems fine, then you've heard your unconscious mind at work, picking up on cues you're not consciously aware of, warning you about them. Or if you've ever been made uncomfortable by someone you've just met, someone who seems friendly enough, then you've heard alarm signals coming from your unconscious mind about contradictions in that person's superficial friendliness masking perhaps some deeper anger or angst.

You should listen to your unconscious mind carefully in those moments, but you should also make friends with it and listen to it much more routinely whenever you want to figure out what someone is intending to do or thinking about doing, whether it's in a meeting or a negotiation or simply a conversation with a friend. You'll find, as you practice your listening skills, that your ability to hear your unconscious quickly and accurately will steadily improve, until it's a regular companion at your side keeping you abreast of what's going on around you with very little (conscious) effort. What you need to do is start deliberate conversations with your unconscious mind. Talk to it. More specifically, ask it questions.

Two key steps make this work, so that you're not just standing around listening for voices in your head and wondering if they're the right ones.

First, there are a limited number of situations where you're in the dark about someone else's true feelings and it's important that you know. So, you can plan those questions in advance. Second, you're going to phrase those questions as polarities, simple yes or no questions, and thus the answers will be clear and simple.

Ask the Right Questions, Get Useful Answers

Start with the basic four I've discussed already:

- Is this person friend or foe?

- Is this person truth telling or lying?

- Is this person on my side or not?

- Is this person powerful or not?

These four questions will cover a great many of the situations where there is some mystery of intent or emotion that needs to be cleared up with a strong reading of body language, because you can't ask directly, you fear some sort of deception, or you want to be sure of the promises or offers being made.

Once you become comfortable asking your unconscious mind these questions, you'll be able to branch out with others. So, for example, let's say you're in the middle of a job interview, and you want to know what the likelihood of getting the job is—at least as far as the interviewer is concerned. You ask yourself, *Is Elizabeth going to hire me or not? Yes or no?* And wait for the answer. It's a combination of friend or foe and alignment, and with your work on both basic questions, you should be able to get a reliable answer without too much trouble.

Let's get comfortable with the technique. It's quite straight-forward. You simply need to pose the question within your mind to yourself, looking at the person and feeling the full weight of the question. So, for example, if your boss promises you a raise if you'll just hang in there a few more months of eighteen-hour days, look at her and ask yourself, *is* _____ *telling me the truth or lying?* Then wait. Keep your mind as blank as possible, and wait for the answer to show up.

If you have any experience with meditation or the Zen Buddhist idea of the empty mind, that will be very helpful.[10] You will know something about having an open, quiet, recep-tive mind. The idea is most emphatically not to chase after an answer at this point, but to let it come to you. That's important.

Understand that your unconscious mind has already picked up a thousand clues for the right answer. You're simply posing the question to that part of you that *already knows the answer.* That gut feeling you had that for some reason the conversation isn't going well? Or that you're knocking the presentation out of the park? Or that the negotiation is about to tip your way? That's your unconscious mind speaking. You're just not used to listening to it, and you haven't asked it the right questions in the right way.

So be patient, wait, and listen for your mind to give you the answer. After a bit, you'll just know. You won't hear voices in your head; rather, you'll just have the new attitude in your mind. When you have that knowledge, then your unconscious mind has spoken, and you can trust it.

Now, this sort of listening takes some honest, clear self-knowledge. If you know about yourself that you are prone to *want* to believe a boss, a spouse, or a friend, then you have to be very careful not to let wish fulfillment speak before your unconscious mind does. And you have to be prepared to get an answer that you don't want.

Learn to Listen to Your Unconscious Mind

You must wait, quieting your conscious mind as much as you can, to allow the whisper from your unconscious mind to inform your thinking. At first, the connection will seem very tenuous, but with practice you'll find yourself hearing your unconscious mind more and more easily and with more and more confidence.

What's happening is that Ekman's micro-expressions and a host of other tiny, constant signals from the other person's body language are coming together to give you a clear reading of what that other person's unconscious mind is telling his or her body to do as a result of an emotion, an attitude, an intent, or a feeling. While most adults, as I've said, are reasonably good at keeping a bland, polite expression on their faces while they're actually thinking something else, they're not very good at controlling the rest of their bodies. Emotions will seep out, in micro-expressions on the face, but more consistently, reliably, and directly, from the rest of the body.

If that other person is concealing some anger, she may be able to compose her face in a neutral or smiling expression, but the tension will get expressed in her shoulders, posture, or hands, and your unconscious mind has already picked that up. You've evolved to be very quick at that kind of unconscious reading of other people; you're just going to train your conscious mind to get better and quicker at interpreting the unconscious messages.

Remember the four basic questions:

- Is this person friend or foe?

- Is this person truth telling or lying?

- Is this person on my side or not?

- Is this person powerful or not?

Once you've practiced and mastered those, then you can branch out to pose additional questions to your unconscious mind. You must always pose them in the form of a yes-or-no choice, because your connection to your unconscious mind is tenuous enough that you can only rely on binary, either/or kinds of readings. But your unconscious mind is awash in the data that you need. It has already taken it all in. You just need to learn to interrogate your own mind in a new way.

Let me stress, once again, that the key is posing a binary question, clearly and simply, and then waiting for the answer. It helps to really want to know. It's as if you were saying to yourself, *Come on, tell me! Is ___ lying or telling the truth? Which is it? I gotta know!* Then, you turn off that conscious mind and just look and wait as powerfully as you can. Be radically open. Let the answer seep into your conscious mind. Take time. Be patient. You already know. Your mirror neurons have already fired in response to the other person inside your head. It's just a matter of seeing, hearing, feeling, and *knowing* what your unconscious already knows.

Human Emotions Are Contagious

Remember, we humans are an empathetic species. Our emotions are contagious. We share them. That means that if you're on edge, excited, angry, happy, sad, or thrilled, or you're suddenly seeing the ridiculous side of the situation, very quickly everyone around will share in that emotion, if it's a strong one.

That's the natural human state, to share emotions with one another. We're most comfortable when we're all on the same wavelength, all in the same mood. It's hard for us to keep secrets from each other.

Perfect sharing doesn't happen as often as it should, because much of the time we're not focused in our emotions or feeling one strongly. So we carry with us a mishmash of conscious and unconscious thoughts, emotions, attitudes, fears, and hopes. None predominate much of the time. As such, the day goes by in a blur, lacking that sense of solidarity or emotional connected or flow state that we only occasionally experience.

That's why strong, focused people and people who are feeling a powerful emotion tend to dominate a discussion, meeting, or situation. Others are swept up because of the human facility for alignment, emotional confluence, and harmony.

We call this groupthink when it causes us to move in lockstep in a certain direction that later proves to be unwise. But, in fact, sharing emotions and intents is the natural extension of our humanity, and most of the time it's not a bad thing at all.

Emotion plays a much more essential role in communication than most of us realize or want to acknowledge. The messiness and unpredictability of emotions make them tricky to handle and contain, especially in professional settings like business presentations, hence, the tendency of (especially) business communicators to shy away from dealing in emotions. Yet research shows that without emotion, it is impossible to remember, let alone listen and act on a communication. Emotion is the glue that holds humans and human communications together.

Emotion is what determines authenticity. More than ever, we demand authenticity of our leaders—the ones we haven't already given up on. So, of course, authenticity is essential in communications.

If you show up unprepared and nervous, even if you mean well, the odds are good that your body language will signal nervousness to the other bodies in the room. People will read you as insincere, unprepared, incompetent, and so on. The unconscious dialogue will already be signaling trouble long before you're consciously ready to try to make a good impression.

The unconscious doesn't make exceptions or give you a break. It doesn't think, *He's just probably a little nervous because it's the beginning of a meeting.* It just thinks, *Oh-oh. Trouble ahead. One of the pack is nervous. In fact, the one who's supposed to be the alpha in charge.* You'll have failed to seem authentic, the fundamental test of leadership, before you've started.

That's why it's so important to prepare adequately for an important speech, meeting, or even conversation. That's why it's so important to be clear about the story you're telling and your emotional attitude toward it. That's why it's so important to be consistent in what I call the two conversations—content and body language.

"Is body language really necessary?" a frustrated executive once asked me. He had his hands full with learning his talk, coping with the technology, and, well, picking out his tie. His question was really, "Do I have to think consciously about my audience's body language—and my own—with everything else I have to do to deliver a great speech to that audience? It's just too much to worry about!"

I was happy to be able to tell him that you shouldn't think *consciously* about other people's body language or your own, under most circumstances; it's a very inefficient way to use your conscious mind. You should think *unconsciously* about body language, however. In fact, you can't help it. Your mind will do that anyway. You might as well make use of it.

Besides, thinking consciously about your body language will slow you down, causing your body language to look fake or insincere to the unconscious minds of the people in your audience, which are faster to pick up information than conscious minds.

Of course, because the conscious mind is so limited in its capacity, trying to drive body language with it will cause it to overload quickly, as my executive did. So, instead, turn over your body language chores—monitoring your own and everyone else's—to your unconscious mind, which is up to the task.

Once you've mastered the basics of this technique, as I indicated, you can move on to other questions and indeed more sophisticated polling of your unconscious mind.

Here's a quick review of the method:

1. *Learn the basic body language constellations.* The four basic issues are: power, friendship, alignment, and lying. Take time to learn the kinds of body language that typically go with each of these issues. Observe each issue at play in turn. Study different people you know well to get a sense of the variety and range of expressions of these various intents. Practice watching people you know well and people you've just met to see the differences.

2. *Decide what you want to know.* This step is critically important, because it's the way you start tapping into your unconscious expertise. What is it that you want to understand about someone else's body language?

Is she lying? Is she the real decision maker? Is he going
to offer you the job? Is he a threat to your career?
Formulate the question in a simple yes-or-no format,
a choice between two poles. Friend or foe? Telling the
truth or lying? On my side or not? Powerful or not?
Those are the basic four. As soon as you've worked
with those enough to feel comfortable with them you
can branch out.

Figure out the question you want to study *before*
you go into the meeting, the interview, or whatever the
situation is, because you're under too much pressure to
pay attention and take part once you're actually in the
moment. This little step—of thinking ahead, figuring
out how the meeting will go, and deciding the question
you want to answer—will pay huge dividends in
awareness as you get the hang of it over time.

3. *Pose the question to your unconscious.* Once you've
   figured out what you want to know, then sit still for
   a moment and pose the question to your unconscious
   mind. Say something like, "In this interview, I want
   to know if Bob is telling me the truth or not?" Focus
   your mind on that and push out other concerns,
   nerves, and distractions.

4. *As the meeting takes place, wait for your unconscious to
   let you know what the answer is.* At first, your unconscious will only whisper its information to you, and it
   will do that slowly. You'll be uncertain about what it's
   telling you. But as you practice, the answers will come
   faster and more clearly.

People who say they have a strong "gut instinct" or "good intuition" are already listening to the messages that their unconscious

minds are sending them. The point is that anyone can learn to develop this sense, just like a muscle. It takes practice, and you must go through each of the steps.

With time, you'll develop this ability to pose questions to your unconscious mind and get the answers back more and more clearly and quickly. Until you have the expertise, don't bet on an inside straight.

FIELD NOTES

Don't Just Read Alignment, Create It

Leadership often involves negotiating very tough deals, handling strong objections, or getting a reluctant team to agree to some difficult course of action. To accomplish such things, we employ all the verbal means at our disposal. We argue, we reason, we cajole, we promise, we wheedle, we make deals. A lot of verbal heavy lifting.

Yet most of us give little thought to our nonverbal actions while these verbal activities are going on. We may consciously raise our voices, use anger to try to carry the day, or even stand up to physically dominate the room. But beyond that, we're clueless about nonverbal means of persuasion.

So it can pay to learn some of the body language of persuasion consciously and employ it carefully in certain situations. Nonverbal persuasion is subtle, it works more slowly, and it works mostly on the unconscious. As such, it can allow all sides to save face and avoid getting too deeply dug into a difficult negotiation. Try the nonverbal argument right from the start. It may save you a lot of time and trouble.

Here are three basic steps for winning the nonverbal argument when emotions are running high. All must be done so subtly they are not consciously noticed.

First, mirror your adversary. Mirroring builds agreement; you can often head off potential trouble by establishing a strong basis of nonverbal agreement before the real negotiating begins. But you mustn't be obvious. The idea is simple enough: when the other party adopts a certain seated or standing position, try to adopt a similar one yourself. You want to move slowly until you more or less match the other person's stance.

The idea is to take some time standing or sitting in roughly the same position as the other person. That will send an unconscious message to the person that you are on an equal level and generally in agreement with him or her. He or she will begin to trust you. But remember not to be obvious about it.

If the person starts arguing, heckling, or violently disagreeing with you, don't mirror; align. Often strong verbal argument comes from a desire to be heard and acknowledged. If you align yourself with the person—that is, sit or stand facing in the same direction—you'll be surprised how often all protest will cease. Alignment looks and feels different from mirroring. With alignment, you stand shoulder to shoulder with someone, looking in the same direction.

This action can be quite difficult to undertake; your natural instinct is to back away from anyone who is heckling you or move in very close to pick a direct fight. But try alignment and watch the confrontation fizzle.

If tension still remains high, use the hands-down gesture to dampen it. When tempers flare and feelings run high, spread your hands out, palms down, at about waist height, and gently push them down a couple of inches. If you're sitting at a table, you'll have to bring your hands above the horizontal plane of the tabletop. Again, this must be done so subtly that it probably isn't consciously noticed. Repeat as necessary. This gesture sends a clear message that it's wise and safe to calm down now.

These gestures won't remove the need for hard verbal bargaining, of course, but they can begin to defuse tense situations more easily. Use the power of your nonverbal messages before you have to resort to verbal fisticuffs.

CHAPTER SUMMARY

- Paul Ekman, the world's foremost expert on lying, has developed a system of reading faces through micro-expressions to tell if people are lying or not.

- The problem with that system is that it takes specialized training, and the results are sometimes ambiguous even with the training.

- So I've developed a simple process that allows you to tap into the power of your unconscious mind to read other people's intent toward you.

- The system covers four important areas of human communication: power, friendship, alignment, and lying.

- There are basic, virtually universal aspects of body language that are helpful to know to make the process work better.

- Once you've learned the basics, practice the system by asking yourself the key question and waiting with an open mind for the answer.

- With time, you'll become quite adept at reading others.

CHAPTER FOUR

Mastering Your Own Voice

The Most Powerful Leadership Cue

Dominance by one person or group over others turns out to be based on something much more mysterious than the obvious things you might imagine, like muscle power or the size of one's military arsenal. It turns out that humans emit low-frequency sounds that align with a leader's similar signals. We are largely unaware—consciously—of what's going on. This chapter will explore the mysteries of social dominance and sound. I'll share the findings of Stanford Gregory and Timothy Gallagher, whose path-breaking work on presidential elections first revealed the significance of these subsonic signals. You'll learn how to use your voice to take control of the room, the meeting, or the situation.

Dune, Vocal Control, and Sounds You Don't Hear

The first power cue prompted you to take a personal body language gestural inventory. The second taught you to begin to control your body language through controlling your emotions—when it matters. The third taught you to use your unconscious expertise to read other people's intents and emotions. Now the fourth power cue will show you how to begin to take control of others with your voice.

In his classic science fiction novel *Dune*, Frank Herbert shows us a powerful family communicating their intent with secret hand signals and controlling less dominant individuals with the Voice, a mysterious way of speaking that bends others to their will.[1]

Here's the surprising truth: you can actually do something like this with your own voice, in real life. By finding and releasing your leadership voice, you can increase your leadership capability enormously. By mastering your own voice, in short, you can begin to master others.

Power Cue 4: Do you have a leadership voice?

Researchers have known for a long time that when we speak, we put out low-frequency sounds that we're not aware of—consciously. We can hear them, dimly, if we focus on them, as a kind of hum, but most of us screen out the sound as not meaningful, so we're not aware of it. The researchers assumed that these noises were meaningless by-products of our vocal chords working away as we communicate with one another and shout at passing cars and other annoyances.[2]

They were wrong. Those sounds are not only meaningful, but they determine who's in charge.

The good news is that you can learn how to increase your production of these secret influencers in order to make sure that you are the leader of any group you want to control.

You can gain mastery of others by using your voice to influence them unconsciously.

The Secret Sounds That Run Your Life

How does this unconscious conversation work, this conversation that you've never before been aware of that runs your life?

Every sound produced by a human—or a musical instrument, an animal, or a machine—has an aural fingerprint that you can measure by charting its frequency responses in units of sound called "hertz." We can hear sounds ranging from twenty hertz at the low end to twenty thousand hertz at the upper end. Anything at about three hundred hertz or lower sounds to us like a low bass note or, as they go lower, not like notes at all, but rather like rumbles of thunder.[3]

It's important to understand that most naturally produced sounds are not pure emissions of one note at one frequency. The quality of a sound—the difference between your mother-in-law's voice, for example, and a chain saw—is determined by the overtones and undertones that the sound produces. A sound gets its quality from the *number* of over- and undertones, as well as the *intensity* of them.

Very broadly speaking, we like sounds that are rich in overtones and (especially) undertones. The "thinner" a sound is, the more likely we are to find it irritating. There's a wide individual variation in the kinds of sounds we find appealing, but on the whole, for example, a thin, nasal voice is less appealing to us than a rich, resonant voice.

Here's the amazing part: people who put out the right kind of sounds—below the range of conscious human hearing—become the leaders of most groups.[4]

So what are these low-frequency sounds we all emit and of which we're not usually aware? Sociologist Stanford Gregory of Kent State University decided to study them a bit more closely. What he found was extraordinary.

Who's Really in Charge Here?

Working with colleague Stephen Webster, Gregory studied interviews on the *Larry King Live* show. He started there simply because he needed a large number of conversations to analyze, but King's interviews with other high-status individuals turned out to reveal more than Gregory had expected.

His research built on the work of a member of the French Resistance who used a machine called a vocoder to analyze voices. That Frenchman, Pierre deLontrey, became familiar with the vocoder during World War II and continued to work with it as a professor at the University of Colorado.

The French Resistance had used the vocoder as a coding device. Invented by Bell Labs, it filtered out certain frequencies of the voice. The coders took the frequencies between 100 and 350 hertz in a human voice recording and filtered them out. Then, they took another frequency in a higher register and mixed them up in accordance with a code. In some cases, they actually translated them into the Navajo language. Then, of course, when the Germans or Japanese received it, it just sounded like random sounds. The code was extremely hard to break because you had to know what frequencies had been removed and scrambled and put them back in the original order.

After the war, deLontrey used the vocoder to analyze conversation. When Gregory met deLontrey, the Frenchman was experimenting with various ways of dissecting the voice in conversation. The vocoder enabled them to take apart a conversation, or take apart human speech, into its constituent frequencies.

Using this device, Gregory and his colleague Webster found that in conversations and meetings, people rapidly match each other's low-frequency sounds. Why? In order to have a productive conversation or meeting, we need to literally be on the same wavelength. As Gregory says, "Without the low-frequency sound, it makes it harder for two people to complete a task. Our research showed that when the lower frequency is eliminated in people's interactions, they're not as able to complete a task in as timely a manner or in as accurate a manner, even though they can hear it very crisply. There's just something about the interaction that they have with the other person that is not complete." Gregory and Webster found that humans need the lower-frequency sounds to add some very important emotional aspects to their communications.[5]

In one experiment, they filtered out the lower-frequency sounds and played the recordings to subjects who were asked to rate their impressions of the speakers, positively or negatively. Without the lower-frequency sounds, subjects rated the speakers more negatively.

That, by the way, is why phone conversations are so much less satisfying that in-person conversations. Of course, the lack of body language input is important too, but phone technology does a poor job of transmitting lower frequencies, so the result is that a phone voice is emotionally unsatisfying.

If you do have to have an important conversation over the phone, a good tip is to smile, even though the person you're speaking to can't see you. We hear emotions in the voice, because facial expressions and emotions both change the shape, length, and therefore sound of the vocal cords. If you smile on the phone, your colleagues will hear the warmth coming through in your voice.

But the power of the low-frequency end of the voice goes even further than that. When Stanford and his colleague dug into the Larry King interviews, they found that *lower-status people match the low-frequency sounds of the higher-status people in the room.*

You might expect that everyone would meet in the middle, but that was not the case. When Larry King was interviewing someone of very high status, he matched the high-status individual's tones. When the interviewee was low status, he or she would match Larry King. The quickest to match Larry was Dan Quayle, the former vice president of the United States.

The conclusion? We not only want to be on the same wavelength, we also want to know who's in charge. So the process of picking a leader has more to do with having the right kind of *voice* than it does having the right ideas or the right physique.

Sorting out who is the most powerful person in the room is an important game that we have used for as long as we have been human because relative status is important to us. This need to defer and assert probably goes back to more primitive times when our lives depended on it.

Now it's more likely to be important when picking sides for a sports team, jockeying for power in a business meeting, determining winners and losers in a negotiation, and picking a new pope.

How We Pick Sides

The point is that there is an unconscious element that is literally beyond our conscious ken. What happens first? And what are the criteria? Gregory and Webster's research indicates that the initial process happens quickly, in the first few minutes of the conversation. We get together, we start talking, and in a couple of minutes, we've unconsciously picked a leader and lined up behind him or her.

So it's hardly the case that much conscious thought has gone into determining who should be top dog. Rather, an important part of our relationships to others is determined, at least in part, unconsciously and with incredible speed.

We do this presumably because we've evolved to because our lives once depended on it. Leadership was a mostly unconscious activity, because the unconscious mind works so much faster than the conscious mind, and because it's the unconscious mind that binds humans together.

We just aren't the rational beings we like to think we are. In this case, we don't even know what the criteria are for the selections we're making. We're not aware of making the choices we make. We just let our unconscious minds do it.

In further research with colleague Will Kalkhoff, Gregory tested the sounds that US presidential candidates make during their debates before the election. Here's the astonishing result: *the amount of dominant sounds made by one candidate over the other predicted accurately the outcome of the upcoming election.*[6] In other words, in effect, the two candidates sorted out who was the winner with their unconscious sounds, and then the country followed along.

Of course, it's quite possible that one candidate, knowing that he was behind in the polls, was deferring to the other candidate, expecting him to win. In effect saying, "I know you're going to win, so I'm going to defer to you in this debate." That chicken-and-egg puzzle isn't solved by the research.

But research Gregory conducted on the debates between Barack Obama and John McCain showed an interesting twist.

McCain dominated in the first two debates and led in the polls. In the third debate, however, McCain dominated for the first three-quarters of the debate, until Obama came on strong and took charge at the end. Of course, as we all know, the results of the election followed that strong Obama close.

So you can challenge initial dominance and come on strong to take over by the end of a debate, meeting, or conference. The research still doesn't definitively address the issue of causality, but it suggests that a decision by Obama at some level changed the outcome of the debate—and possibly the election.

The Advantages of a Deep Voice

In any case, the chicken-and-egg question doesn't change the power of this research. What it shows is that people sort themselves out in terms of power very quickly after they meet, within minutes and unconsciously, and they signal that power relationship to each other with their low-frequency vocal patterns.

It further shows that you can shift the pattern if you can come on strong at the end or even work on your vocal production to be powerful from the start.

By the way, this research is consistent with a study that found that, in presidential elections of the past hundred years, the deeper-voiced candidate won every time.[7] Deeper voices confer an advantage, but that doesn't mean women don't have a shot at commanding a room. Gregory says, "In order to speak, we *all* have to use both the lower frequency and the higher frequency." The basic note that we produce is called the fundamental frequency, and it's then surrounded with both higher and lower overtones.

Gregory continues,

It's the fundamental frequency that's generated by the larynx. What is called the super-laryngeal vocal track, that part of our anatomy after the larynges, the pharynx, and so forth, as well as the tongue and the sinuses, and so on, gives tone to a voice. And that's what gives a certain quality to everyone's voice and obviously differences between male and female voices. The female voice has a higher pitch generally because the larynges are not as long. With males the larynges are longer and thus they have a lower pitch. But it really doesn't matter when it comes to the actual speech because speech is created by the energy of the laryngeal tone. It's after that that we put other qualities in it and that gives us a specific tonal quality.

I've seen the potential for anyone to develop a strong leadership voice in my own research and work with clients. Repeatedly, through the years, I have seen people develop strong leadership voices and win over audiences, control meetings, and persuade others. People with thin, nasal voices, on the other hand, turn other people off, don't get listened to, and frequently find themselves at the bottom of the pecking order.

I first saw the power of the voice when I was working with a lawyer who was preparing for a multimillion-dollar case involving a wrongful termination suit. The lawyer was smart and knew exactly what to do in the trial. But I could see that he wasn't going to make any headway with the jury because his voice was whiny and unpleasant. The sound was going to turn the jury off, not sway it in his client's favor. So I gave the lawyer a crash course in vocal production. We worked for a couple of hours a day for several weeks, until his voice—and his authority—was transformed. He won the case.

You're probably wondering, if there's an unconscious conversation going on, how can you master the dialogue? How can you make sure that you're the one who ends up in charge?

The answer is that it's a two-step process. First, you have to develop a leadership voice by some hard, physical work on your vocal production. That's what this fourth power cue is all about. Second, you have to get control of your unconscious dialogue with yourself in order to project a confident "I'm the one in charge here" attitude to the outside world so that it comes out in your voice. I'll focus on that step in chapter 6.

Like most of the steps along the journey to leadership, mastery of the voice is both psychological and physical. You have to get the right story going in your own head, and you have to tell that to the rest of the world using physical means—your body language, vocal chords, unconscious physical messages.

In this chapter, you're just going to work on your voice. You'll learn how to produce a strong voice and then how to pitch that voice in a way that signals leadership. In further chapters, I'll get into the detail of the conversation your unconscious mind has with your body to produce leadership (or its absence) so that you can master the entire package.

Producing the Voice: It's All about Breathing

Most of us don't think about how we produce our voices at all. It's completely unconscious. That makes sense; the unconscious mind is far more powerful and more capable of multitasking than the conscious mind.

But you're going to have to become conscious about how you produce your voice for a while, because what you want is one of those rich, resonant, leader-style voices that everyone else lines up behind. You want to add the overtones and especially the undertones that are missing now because you're not supporting your voice with breath.

Your voice, as you now produce it unconsciously, is most probably weak, ineffective, hard for others to listen to, and bad for your own health and thinking. Why? Most of us spend a good deal of our days sitting in front of computers, with our bodies bent at the waist. It's very hard to get a full lungful of air in this position, and it takes a full lungful in order to get the kind of resonance we need.

As a result, most people's voices are thin and nasal. Not the stuff of leadership. In fact, quite the opposite. Most importantly, this sort of voice doesn't send out the lower-frequency sounds that command leadership. In work with clients, I have heard their voices improve measurably with the techniques outlined here. As a result, they have increased their interpersonal authority and leadership significantly.

When most of us breathe, we lift our shoulders, further squashing our lungs, so that we get little additional help there. Instead, stand up, relax the shoulders, and relax your belly. Now, as you breathe in, take the air in through your belly. Expand your stomach with the air as it comes in. Your shoulders should not move. The only part of you that moves should be your belly, and that should move outward, not up.

Once your stomach is full of air, then tense your abdominal muscles as if you were about to be hit in the stomach and you were bracing for the blow. Now, slowly breathe out by squeezing your stomach muscles in and gradually moving your belly toward your back. If you know what an eyedropper is, imagine one. The bulb is your stomach, and you expand it to take in air, just as you would take in liquid into the eyedropper by letting the bulb expand. Then, to squeeze out the medicine, you squeeze the bulb. The stomach works the same way with air, like a bellows. Expand to take in air, squeeze down to push air out through your mouth and nose, producing sound.

That's diaphragmatic breathing, or belly breathing, and it's the way operatic tenors hit high Cs and Beyonce's voice reportedly spans five octaves when most of us can barely manage two.[8]

Now Speak

Belly breathing has all kinds of health benefits in addition to the leadership voice you're concerned with here, so it's something you should practice several times a day anyway. But especially when you're getting ready to speak, expand that belly, tense the abdominals, and slowly squeeze the air out of your stomach while beginning to speak. With a little practice, this motion will become second nature to you, and your vocal resonance will increase.

But there's a little more to it. Not only do you have to increase the low-frequency sounds with better voice production, you have to let them out by relaxing your jaw, opening your mouth, and letting your vocal chords achieve their full power.[9]

So practice the breathing, and then practice speaking (in private) in order to let your voice out. This combination of tension (of the diaphragm and stomach) and relaxation (of the jaw, throat, and vocal chords) is quite tricky to achieve, because most of us have learned over the years to do the opposite, but it is essential to bring the voice out—the leadership voice.

Tension of all kinds makes this more difficult. If you're worried about something, tense physically, or distracted, all of that will make it harder to relax your mouth and throat and tense your stomach to produce a great, leadership-ready sound.

If you're having difficulty achieving the right result, lie flat on your back, relax your jaw, mouth, neck, and vocal chords, and then breathe in by inflating your stomach. At first, try making simple noise—only when you exhale—keeping your mouth open and relaxed the entire time. Say something like "fa-fa-fa-fa," kicking your stomach in on each syllable.

Once you've mastered this, try saying words and phrases, gradually lengthening them until you can speak, ideally for up to thirty to forty-five seconds on a breath, with a resonant tone that carries.

Have you ever heard someone who can make his voice carry throughout a large room with no apparent effort? It is this diaphragmatic voice that makes that feat possible.

That's the first step. There's a second step that's equally important. This is the step that produces the leadership magic. And you're going to need a piano.

Pitching Your Voice to Project Leadership

Every voice has something called the maximum resonance point (MRP). You can find your own, if you're not tone deaf and have access to a keyboard. Determine the lowest note you can comfortably hum and the highest. I've found that, for people who are not musically trained, starting at middle C is helpful, because it's a note most people can find and hum. (Men, don't use your falsetto range for this purpose. Women, don't use your "head voice," the female equivalent of falsetto.[10])

Next, count the number of white notes on the keyboard you span. Divide that number by four and then count that many notes up from the bottom of your range. That note is your maximum resonance point.

Why is that important? Because all sorts of good things happen at that point. Most simply, resonance is pleasing to their ears, so people will respond favorably to your voice. Second, your voice is happiest at that pitch, so it will last longer than if you try to speak higher or lower habitually. Men often try to speak lower than their MRP, and women sometimes go higher. The result is a strangled tone that pleases no one, puts strain on the voice, and causes long-term damage.

I've worked with so many people who have damaged their voices—and thus inadvertently their leadership potential—by speaking habitually at pitches that are too high or too low. Over time, the vocal chords lose their flexibility and range if they're not properly supported through breathing, and that shows up in a less appealing and less commanding voice.

But there's more. The MRP is where you put out the most overtones and undertones—especially undertones—that give you the best chance to take over leadership of your group. This is the Ronald Reagan presidential voice, the voice that says, *Relax, I'm in charge, don't worry. Everything is going to turn out fine.*

A bathroom with all its hard porcelain surfaces is a good place to practice working on your MRP. To find the right voice tone, practice moving up and down through your vocal range until you find that pitch that seems to echo throughout your head and the room. That's the pitch that maximizes the subsonic frequencies and will thus enhance your leadership power.

To see how this works in practice, study—yes—President Ronald Reagan's voice. It's a perfect leader's voice; it oozes resonance and authority with every phrase. Reagan was a trained actor from the old days of the studios in Hollywood, and he was a radio presence for a number of years. The combined experiences and training gave him a voice destined to lead.[11]

That's what you need. Not the years on radio or in Hollywood, but the resonance that will give your voice authority.

As you listen to Reagan, notice how he varied his pitch, but kept returning to his home base, his MRP, especially when he was saying something really important. You need the vocal variety, of course, to sustain interest, but you need to use your MRP to create the leadership voice and control.

Gregory notes, "Actors can more consciously manipulate their voices by putting themselves in an emotional place," so we can conclude that politician Reagan often called upon the training that actor Reagan had received. Gregory points out further, "The lower-frequency sounds are processed mostly in the right hemisphere, while the higher-frequency sounds are processed in the left hemisphere" of the brain. That correspondence indicates that lower frequencies are likely to be more closely linked to the emotions and the higher frequencies to the logical, left-brain thinking. That, of course, is consistent with research, as I've indicated earlier, that shows that decision making is largely emotional (and right brain). But then most of us would admit that our decisions to follow one leader or another, or one political party or another, are mostly emotional decisions.

Gregory adds, "The easiest way to understand this lower frequency is with singing. Part of the idea in singing is to manipulate the larynges to emphasize that lower frequency. And what people don't usually understand is that even though normal speech is not singing, we're still manipulating that lower frequency, in essentially an emotional way, rather than the more conscious way that is associated with the higher frequency of normal speaking." The manipulation of the lower frequency in singing is why singing is so much more immediately emotional for humans than talking.

It's those emotionally powerful low-frequency sounds that translate into a leadership presence. Gregory comments, "There are various ways people show their status. Very often, they're introduced—you know the president is coming, or the department chair is coming, or your boss. But sometimes you don't know that. And there are people who just seem to have this commanding presence and you tend to defer to them."

As Gregory is at pains to point out, humans need to establish a pecking order in order to communicate well and work well together: "For the most part, under normal circumstances, you know how to place yourself in the hierarchy. And by doing that, you're able to communicate better. We are animals. If you observe animals, you find that the pecking order is a really important thing to establish before you get anything done."

How do you seize control if you want to be the leader? Gregory says, "The best way to establish dominance is to be prepared. And to be confident. Another way is to be bogus and act like you are. But in the long run that doesn't work."

Now Speak Authoritatively

There's one other thing your voice needs: the authoritative arc.

All of your work on vocal production and resonance will be useless without this last aspect of your voice. Many people speak as if every sentence were a question? That is, they raise their voices slightly in pitch at the end of every phrase or sentence?

They do this probably because they're seeking agreement, but the result is both incredibly annoying and lacks authority. There is simply no way you can take charge of a meeting, your colleagues, or your career if you have this verbal tic.

I see it most with women in business, and with both men and women in businesses with a heavy emphasis on being collegial. But however it happens, you must fight it. Instead, begin your phrase or sentence at your normal pitch, allow it to rise during the sentence to show passion and energy, then bring it back down by the end to show authority.

This simple little trick alone has transformed the professional lives of some clients that I've worked with. One in particular was offered a promotion to vice president, quit her job, and started her own company advising the organization she had worked for and others like it after I worked with her on the authoritative arc.

To see what I mean, study Martin Luther King Jr.'s "I Have a Dream" speech. That speech, considered one of the best of the twentieth century, perfectly exemplifies both the authority and the passion that the voice can project. It changed the world. In it, King soars up on lines like, "I have a dream that my four little children will one day live in a nation where they will not be judged by the color of their skin but by the content of their character." At the end, he comes down back to his original starting pitch, and the result is powerful, persuasive, and authoritative.

Don't Undermine Your Newly Developed Authority

This chapter has focused on *how* you speak, not what you're saying. I'll get to content later, after you've learned how to control the much more influential unconscious parts of communication. However, I do want to address one aspect of what you say here: verbal tics.

Some people say "like" and "you know" so often that you want to strangle them. Others say "um" often and enthusiastically.

Some people swallow nervously and spasmodically. Some people let their voices swing up in pitch at the end of every sentence as if they were always asking questions. For some, it's happy *feet*—wandering around the stage as if they really loved walking and couldn't wait to get off the platform.

I've seen a thousand tics over my years as a speech coach, and I've had a thousand people come up to me and point out someone else's tic, usually in whispered tones, along with, "Can't you fix them?" Here's the thing about tics. Of course, we're better off without them, but they're not really a problem unless an audience notices them and they get in the way of comprehension.

Then we do have a problem, Houston. And it's time to get out the Taser and fix it. A few shocks later, and your tic is gone. Just kidding. There are several relatively painless ways to fix a tic. My favorite is to get someone, a friend, to count the tics over some specified period of time, like a speech, and then charge the offender an agreed-upon sum for each offense. Usually a dollar is enough to get the malefactor's attention. And you'd be astonished how quickly the tic goes away after you've had to pay up a couple of times.

Another method is to videotape the speaker and point out the tics. That's usually enough for the speaker to want to stop, and wanting to stop is usually enough to allow him or her to do so.

If you're one of those people who says "like" or "you know" or "um" and you're aware of it, then self-monitoring may be the simplest way to fix the problem. Notice yourself in a relatively low-stress situation—say, a conversation—and just stop talking when the urge to "um" comes over you. Don't stop forever, just long enough to let a little pause in your conversation flow rather than the tic. You'll be surprised at how quickly you can train yourself to do without the "likes" or "you knows" or "ums." They just go away.

So let's all calm down about tics and start quietly eliminating them on our own. I'll have less to do as a coach, but that's OK.

By the way, don't try to do any fixing of tics under the gun, when you're facing a deadline for an important presentation or meeting. You've got too much else going on; it won't stick. Wait for a calm period of your work life. Changing behavior like this takes a minimum of three weeks, so be prepared to work at it for a while.

That's how you develop your leadership voice. Change your breathing, your voice production, and the authority of your voice. Eliminate any tics that are undercutting that authority. The goal is to let your leadership voice out from where it has been trapped inside you. Do this and you will change your leadership journey. There are a few more steps involved, but if you can master this step, you're well on the way to taking charge of your life—and becoming a natural leader. You'll find more details on how to develop and maintain your leadership voice in the field notes at the end of this chapter.

Go Back to the Source

If you're musical or theatrical—or if you're just particularly interested in developing your voice—I recommend the work of Patsy Rodenburg. If Paul Ekman is the god of lies and lying, Rodenburg is the goddess of voice. She's worked with many great actors and directors, including Judi Dench, Ian McKellen, Antony Sher, Richard Eyre, and Mike Nichols. She was the voice coach for the Royal Shakespeare Company for a decade. She's figured out a couple of essential things about your voice that will help you become charismatic and change the world.

She's written a number of books on the subject of charisma and the voice. Of those, I particularly recommend *The Right to*

Speak and *Presence*.[12] But most of all, if you need to communicate as part of your job or your life, you should begin doing her vocal exercises and breathing work every day.

Rodenburg's work involves helping people bring out their full voices in order to increase their presence and charisma. Until you've done the work, it's a little hard to understand, but most people don't speak with their full voices. Because of shyness, attitude, emotional scars—you name it—what comes out is only a partial representation of their full personality. I've worked with clients using Rodenburg techniques, and it's powerfully moving to hear the full voice come out after years of repression.

Rodenburg's other big idea is also connected with charisma. She describes three kinds of presence: first circle, second circle, and third circle, to use her terminology. First-circle people are introverted or self-absorbed, and when they are talking to others, they focus their energy inward. Third-circle people are bombastic or bullies, and they focus their energy outward in order to dominate. Second-circle people (hint—this is where you want to be) have the right balance between self-awareness and presence for others.

It's a compelling concept when it's applied and a great way to understand charisma and presence. Rodenburg is indeed the goddess of voice.

The Leadership Conversation

Remember, every communication is two conversations. The two must be aligned in order for you to be effective. Your message must be clear. But your second conversation, a combination of all the unconscious signals you send out and that are received by your listeners, must be powerful too. Leaders can't afford to speak with diffidence, ambivalence, or confusion for long. If their nonverbal conversation reveals their uncertainty, that feeling will quickly spread to everyone around them. And that begins with what people hear in your voice.

Many leaders learn to develop a leadership voice unconsciously by having an early success, feeling more confident, and then carrying themselves more confidently as a result. That improved posture naturally creates a stronger voice.

But I've also seen the opposite happen. A psychological blow or a setback can lead to emotional tensions and issues that show up in body language and in voice.

When the career goes well, the leader overcomes these setbacks and gets back on the ascending track. Then, as he or she moves up through the ranks, getting increasing responsibilities and power, his or her unconscious mind follows along, believing more strongly with each success, and then projecting through the voice (and body language) that belief.

Now, with the techniques I've taught you here, you can short-circuit that learning process and become strong leadership material with a few months of regular practice. You can be ready for leadership when it comes your way.

Leaders over the years have confessed after the fact to doubts about some important decisions, doubts that they were able to conceal at the time. Churchill, for example, knew many nights of indecision, uncertainty, and anguish during World War II, yet he was careful not to let that show during his radio broadcasts and speeches to the House of Commons. How fortunate for England that it had a leader who was able to radiate confidence even during that country's darkest hours.[13]

The art of persuasion depends on consistency in message from both conversations. That means successful leaders have to learn how to control and align the two when it counts. It begins with the voice. Lives may literally depend on that control.

Maintaining Your Voice

Finding your leadership voice is particularly important for anyone who regularly speaks in public. But if you're a speaker, you'll need to do more than just master your voice; you'll need to maintain it.

As a public speaker, you thrive—or are mute—because of your voice. The research is only beginning to reveal how much depends on the way we hear each other's voices, but it is clear that voices convey surprising amounts of information about themselves and their owners. A recent study suggests that (men's) voices give us a fairly accurate assessment of their owners' upper-body strength, for example.[14]

The care and feeding of your voice is therefore incredibly important for your long-term success. Following is a five-step program for getting the most out of your voice and using it to propel your career success over the long term.

1. Find That Maximum Resonance Point

As I've indicated, there is an optimal pitch for every voice. Make sure you find yours, because voices at their maximum resonance point are most pleasing and persuasive to others.

If you pitch your voice lower or higher than that habitually, you'll put strain on your vocal chords and damage them over time.

2. Support That Voice and Increase Its Natural Resonance with Good Belly Breathing

Because we are sitting at computers for the greater part of the day, most of us breathe through our upper chests. That tends to make our voices nasal, not resonant. Nasal voices are unpleasant to listen to and unpersuasive.

To fight this problem, stand up and breathe in through your stomach, expanding it with air. Then tense the diaphragmatic muscles and let the air trickle out slowly through your mouth as you speak. Singers call this "supporting" the voice. With good support, your voice not only will sound more resonant and thus more pleasing and persuasive, but will also last longer.

You'll also find that this belly breathing calms you when you get an attack of adrenaline before a speech. Take three or four deep belly breaths before you walk on stage, and both you and your voice will benefit. Remember to breathe again during the course of the speech, and you'll benefit even more.

3. Retain a Touch of the Nasal Voice So You Can Be Heard

Nasal voices are intensely irritating, but resonant voices with just a touch of the nasal are both delightful and able to be heard. A voice with no nasal quality at all is difficult to detect from background noise, and it lacks conviction. We call this nasal touch "presence," and all voices need presence.

4. Let Your Real Voice Out

Now that you've taken care of the technical aspects of voice production, you need to let your voice be heard in the larger sense. Allow your voice to rise with passion and fall with authority, like Martin Luther King Jr.'s voice patterns in his "I Have a Dream" speech. Don't swallow your voice or hold back your emotions. Your voice—your breath—was once believed to be intimately connected with your soul. Let it out and be heard. Why else get up to speak?

Technically, to deliver a great sound, keep your head up and speak to the back row, opening your mouth and bringing the sound forward. Never swallow your voice, as too many Americans, especially men, do. That damages the vocal chords and gives the voice a gravely quality that is unpleasant and grating. More than that, it is the physical manifestation of emotion being held in check, which audiences will interpret as insincere, inauthentic, or simply boring.

5. Have a Conversation with Your Audience, but an Elevated One

The genre of public speaking today is casual. We respond better to people who talk to us informally rather than reading a speech or declaiming in the style of fifty or sixty years ago. But that's no excuse for a lack of clarity, for a plethora of "ums" and "ahs," or for mumbling.

Speak clearly, vary the pace, finish one sentence before jumping to the next, and generally speak cleanly. Listening to a speech or presentation is hard work for an audience; it's hard to remember what we've heard. Make it easy on your audience by speaking clearly, forcefully, and memorably.

CHAPTER SUMMARY

- We all emit low-frequency sounds when we speak that determine our leadership presence.

- We defer unconsciously to leaders who have stronger low-frequency sounds.

- You can learn to increase the leadership potential of your voice through breathing and other vocal exercises, and practicing the authoritative arc.

CHAPTER FIVE

Communicating as a Leader

Combining Voice and Body Language for Success

Researchers at MIT have figured out how to predict the success of an entrepreneurial pitch to venture capitalists with astonishing accuracy, without even hearing the details of the pitch itself. Unspoken signals—posture, pacing, pauses—all can be measured and reliably predict success and failure. In this chapter, I look at the so-called "honest signals" and suggest how to maximize them for success.

Can You Accurately Determine Personal Success or Failure Based on Social Signals?

It's the nerds' revenge. MIT researchers have figured out that, in lead researcher Sandy Pentland's words, "People have a second channel of communication that revolves not around words but around *social relations*. This social channel profoundly influences major decisions in our lives *even though we are largely unaware of it.*" Indeed, Pentland has made it his cause to show the world "how powerful and pervasive this form of communication is in our daily lives, how it changes the way we think of ourselves and our organizations, and how you can make use of this information to better manage your life."[1]

Power Cue 5: What honest signals do you send out in key work and social situations?

Pentland is talking about body language, the second conversation, with all the evangelical enthusiasm of the converted, in this case of a converted engineer who had hitherto focused on the verbal content of what other people said to him and around him. He goes on, "What we have found is that many types of human behavior can be reliably predicted from biologically based, *honest signaling* behaviors. These ancient primate signaling mechanisms, such as the amount of synchrony, mimicry, activity, and emphasis, form an unconscious channel of communication between people."

What's different and intriguing about Pentland's work, though, is that he has gone beyond most researchers on body language to use behavior as a predictive tool. His ability to do so comes from his rejection of the old approach to body language that I discussed earlier, the attempt to catalog an encyclopedia of gestures with one-to-one meanings. Instead, Pentland and his team focused on patterns of behavior, constellations of nonverbal activity that, taken together, prove to be reliable and meaningful predictors of human intent and attitude.

Pentland notes, "These social signals are not just a back channel or complement to our conscious language; they form a separate communication network that powerfully influences our behavior. In fact, these honest signals provide a quite effective window into our intentions, goals and values. By examining this ancient channel of communication, for instance—paying no attention to words or even who the people are—we can accurately *predict* outcomes of dating situations, job interviews, and even salary negotiations."

They're Honest Because They Tell the Truth

So what are these honest signals? Pentland calls them "honest" because he wants to convey the idea that nonverbal signals and patterns of behavior, unlike words, are largely truthful, revealing our real intentions. We learn to lie with words, as I've said, and even with our faces, but our overall nonverbal communications are very hard to fake.

The four honest signals, or patterns of behavior, are:

Influence—how much one person dominates the conversation.

Mimicry—how much one person mirrors another.

Activity—how energetic a person is.

Consistency—how even-keeled a person is.

Let's see what each one involves. *Influence* means the extent to which you dominate the conversation, in the sense that other people copy your patterns of speech and unconsciously defer to you. That's pretty clear: you've probably got to do most of the talking—at least 51 percent, on the whole, which suggests that you have to do your homework, know what you're talking about, and have some passion for the subject. Faking that will be difficult in the long run.

But it's more complicated than that, isn't it? We've all encountered people who say less, but what they say matters more—people who know how to use silence to dominate an exchange. So having influence must mean more than just doing all the talking. The issue is all about taking charge in some deeper way than just talk. As Pentland says, "Influence is measured by the extent to which one person causes the other person's pattern of speaking to match their own pattern."

Which only raises another question: how do you accomplish that?

Mimicry denotes how much mirroring of each other's body language is going on. This one is interesting. If you're appearing before a panel of venture capitalists, for example, you might want to start out mirroring the body language of the most important people on the board. That will make them unconsciously believe that you're a good, trustworthy person. After you've mirrored them for a while, then you want to start *leading*—getting them to mirror you. If you've made a strong impression on them and they like what they're hearing, they will. If not, you'll know right away, because they'll adopt body language stances that are at odds with yours. Our bodies signal what we're thinking before we're consciously aware of it.

So what do you do if you notice that the people you're trying to impress aren't mimicking you back?

Activity indicates the level of energy a person has. So go in with some energy and enthusiasm. Avoid the classic mistake that inexperienced speakers make, which is to lose all affect—the face becoming expressionless—because of the adrenaline coursing through your system. It's an old evolutionary trick; the mind focuses on the important stuff when you're in danger, like increasing your mental alertness and heart rate, but it neglects your facial expressions, because those don't matter much when you're fleeing a woolly mammoth. Because facial expression is one way that people judge activity in others, you don't want to become the great stone face when you're pitching something vital, whether it's a date, a price, or a company. But be aware that the rest of your body matters, too. If you're slumped, and your posture and other gestures indicate a low activity level, grinning from ear to ear constantly won't save you. Your whole body has to be involved, and that is difficult to fake. That's why the work of the first four steps is so important to get right before attempting this step in brain mastery.

But where's the line between good energy and manic enthusiasm? Surely, that's not powerful, is it? How do you know what is the right level of activity?

Consistency has to do with how even keeled you are during the course of the meeting. As Pentland says, "When there are many different thoughts or emotions going on in your mind at the same time, your speech and even your movements become jerky, unevenly accented and paced. The consistency of emphasis and timing is a signal of mental focus, while greater variability may signal an openness to influence from others."

The reason this particular sign is important to our unconscious minds is best illustrated with an example. Let's say you're in the middle of an important negotiation, and the other side throws you a lowball figure. You get flustered, and your previously smooth conversational tone and pace become temporarily erratic as you attempt to figure out what to say next. That demonstrates a lack of consistency, and it means that you will be less likely to succeed in your efforts. Consistency is an important measure of how cool you are, in effect, and we all know that the cool kids tend to win.

But when should you keep an even keel and when should you show some passion, anger, or enthusiasm for a cause? Again, where's the right balance between strength and passion in consistency?

Finally, how do you consistently generate these four honest sets of signals? Especially when it matters, during a sales pitch, a key presentation, or a meeting with the executive team about the future of the organization? At the heart of the matter is confidence, if, like most people, you're unconscious of what's going on. People who believe that they will be successful send out the right unconscious messages, and people who believe that they will fail—whether consciously or unconsciously— find that, indeed, they do fail.

But it's more than just confidence, obviously. Plenty of confident people have failed to win the bid, contract, prize, or race. What happens if you frankly lack confidence? Can you fake it 'til you make it?

Turning Honest Signals into Power Cues

Let's go a little deeper into the science and practice of Pentland's signals and see how they really work. Let's turn them into power cues.

Let's start with influence. There are really four important aspects to what Pentland is talking about that he doesn't fully tease apart. First of all, there's the unmistakable dominance in a conversation such as one I remember with vivid clarity when the chief of staff, David McCloud, reamed me out in very colorful language because I had bypassed him and gone straight to the governor (of Virginia, Chuck Robb) with an idea on how to write a speech. I was still the new speechwriter; I'd been on the staff only a month or two. I had come from the academic world; I had been the assistant vice president and provost at the University of Virginia, with a PhD in literature and rhetoric from that school.

So, of course, I thought I knew better than the chief of staff, who had worked with Robb for years and had engineered a brilliant campaign and election victory, not to mention proved his worth as a speechwriter some years earlier. My month of experience wasn't much, compared to that depth of political experience, but it was long enough for me to think I knew better than McCloud.

I made an appointment with the governor, explained my idea to him, and listened as he gave me a noncommittal answer. Then, I listened again when McCloud, having been informed by the governor of my bypass of the hierarchy, called me into his office for some clarifying remarks.

McCloud proceeded to explain to me—in the earthiest language I'd ever heard—what an idiot I was. He "ripped me a new one" in the current parlance. He was so good at his job that I was simultaneously reduced to a small pile of jelly and awed by his performance. He had passion, he had a command of the language, and he dominated the conversation. I don't think I got a word in edgewise for twenty minutes—and then the conversation was over.

That was influence of a particular kind—the dominance that comes from authority, experience, and the unshakable conviction that you're right and the other fellow is a fool.

Nobody overhearing that conversation would have been in any doubt as to who had influence over whom. That conversation was all about anger; it was a dressing down.

It illustrates two of the four aspects of influence that are essential to understand—and to master—if you want to succeed as a leader. First, positional power. Second, emotion.

Influence Has Four Sources

Take positional power. If you have it, influence becomes a relatively simple proposition. People with power over others tend to talk more, interrupt more, and guide the conversation more, by picking the topics, for example.

If you don't have the positional power in a particular situation, then expect to talk less, interrupt less, and choose the topics of conversation less. After all, exercising their right to talk more about the subjects they care about is one of the ways that people with positional power demonstrate it.

What do you do if you want to challenge the positional authority? Perhaps you have a product, an idea, or a company you want to sell, and you have the ear of someone who can buy it. How do you get control in that kind of situation?

The second aspect of influence is emotion, and using it is one way to counteract positional power and generally to dominate a conversation. In the example above, McCloud had both positional power and emotion, so he steamrollered me. I had no chance. I think I lost five pounds in that twenty-minute one-sided conversation from just sitting and sweating.

But when the other side has the power and you have the emotion, something closer to parity is possible. Indeed, passion can sweep away authority, when it's well supported and the speaker is well prepared. We've all witnessed that happen when an unknown young performer disarms and woos the judges, devastating the competition in one of those talent competitions. The purity and power of the emotion in the performance is enough to silence—and enlist—the judges despite their positional authority. Indeed, the impassioned speech, the plea for clemency, the summation to the jury that brings them to tears and wins the case for the defendant—this is the stuff of Hollywood climaxes.

Passion often links with expertise, the third aspect of influence. Indeed, you can dominate the conversation, beating out positional power, if you have both passion and expertise. The diffident expert's voice is sometimes lost in the clamor of people wanting to be heard. So expertise without passion is not always effective, but if it's patient, it can be the last person standing in a debate and thereby get its turn.

The final aspect of influence is the subtlest of the four and, as such, rarely can trump either positional authority or passion. But in rare instances, artfully manipulated, I have seen it prevail. What is it? It is the mastery of the dance of human interaction.

Can You Control the Conversation—Effortlessly?

We have very little conscious awareness of this aspect of influence, but we are all participants in it with more or less expertise. We learn at a very early age that conversation is a *pas de deux*, a game that two (or more) people play that involves breathing, winking, nodding, eye contact, head tilts, hand gestures, and a whole series of subtle nonverbal signals that help both parties communicate with one another.

Indeed, conversation is much less functional without these nonverbal signals. That's why phone conversations are nowhere near as satisfying as in-person encounters and why conference calls inevitably involve lots more interruptions, miscues, and cross-talking. We're not getting the signals we're used to getting to help us know when the other person is ready to hand the conversational baton on to us, and vice versa.

Can you manage influence using only this fourth aspect? I have seen it done in certain situations, but the other three aspects will usually trump this one. Nonetheless, I once watched a senior executive effortlessly dominate a roomful of people who were ostensibly equal—a group of researchers gathered from around the world to discuss the future of IT. Within a few minutes, everyone in the room was unconsciously deferring to this executive, even though he had no positional power and was not particularly passionate about the subject. His mastery of the subtle signals of conversational cuing was profound, and soon he had everyone dancing to his verbal beat. It was beautiful to watch; he showed complete conversational mastery in action.

Influence, then, is a measure of how much skin the participants have in the game, and most of us are unconscious experts at measuring it. To wield it, you need to have the edge in at least one of its four aspects and preferably more than one.

Let's Understand Mimicry

The second so-called honest signal is mimicry, perhaps the most important one of the four in your quest to master the power cues of human interaction.

This one is key and is relatively easy to master. When I was teaching at Princeton, I trained one student who showed particular interest in this technique. She became the only student in the history of that institution who was offered both the Rhodes and Fulbright scholarships. To be sure, she was smart and well prepared, and I trained her in several additional techniques, but mirroring was the one we focused on, and she used it brilliantly. What did she do so well and how can you use it to improve your leadership skills and power cues?

Humans—and indeed primates in general—copy one another unconsciously when they agree with them, feel comfortable with them, or want to show solidarity with them. Most of us are completely unaware of this behavior at the conscious level most of the time. Like so many other body language signals, we leave the management of mirroring to our unconscious minds. It's simply more efficient.

Yet, when you become aware of mirroring behavior, you'll see it everywhere, and you'll begin to understand how the best salespeople persuade customers so effortlessly, how the most successful politicians bind voters to them despite the issues, and how the most powerful executives build trust among their direct reports and colleagues.

Mirroring reflects alignment, which you learned to read in chapter 3. When we're aligned with someone, we mirror their behavior, and vice versa. When you meet someone for the first time, if you like them and begin to trust them, you'll demonstrate that affinity with mirroring. You may demonstrate it in other ways as well, but mirroring is probably the most reliable indicator of the growing bond between you.

One of the first things that old friends, colleagues who like each other, and acquaintances who feel comfortable with one another do is mirror each other. Unconsciously it sends the message: *I like you. I trust you. I'm aligned with you. You can trust me. You can relax; we're on the same side.*

One of the most entertaining illustrations of mirroring comes when watching two lovers talking in a restaurant or walking down the street, pausing occasionally to look into a shop window. You'll see them mirroring each other's behavior effortlessly and perfectly. It's two bodies moving as one.

Mirroring Is an Important Tool in
Your Power Cue Toolkit

So, of course, mirroring is an important power cue and an important step to master in becoming a powerful leader and communicator. In Pentland's research, for example, adding mimicry to a sales pitch made it 20 percent more effective.

Here's how you do it. It takes several steps. Begin by letting the other person do most of the talking, and instead of trying to dominate the conversation, watch the other person and gradually begin to imitate his or her body positioning and posture. Follow his or her movements, with a delay of a couple of seconds, but do it easily, subtly, and smoothly. If you try to move too much or in unusual ways, or you move too rapidly, you'll draw attention to what you're doing and the other person will feel mocked rather than mirrored.

It's very important to get it right. Don't overdo it. Err on the side of less rather than more, and don't reach too far. It's better to mirror less than too exactly or too quickly.

Once you've established a clear pattern of mirroring, over a period of, say, fifteen or twenty minutes in an hour-long interview, then begin to lead instead of mirroring. You should see the other person mirror you. If you see that behavior, that means you've successfully established trust and a bond with that person, and he or she has ceded control of the conversation to you. He or she trusts you.

Keep leading for fifteen or twenty minutes, and then ask for the sale, make your pitch, or close the deal. Your new colleague will find it very hard to resist you. Pentland found that, in new employee salary negotiations, mimicry accounted for up to a third of the salary variation from one offer to another.

In other words, you can get a 33 percent salary bump simply by mirroring your potential boss.

Mirroring pays.

How to Demonstrate Activity without Looking Crazy

Activity is the third honest signal. Just like a kid at her birthday party, slightly lunatic with excitement at the prospect of all that cake and all those presents, adults still fidget more, talk more, and talk faster when they're interested in something or someone. Because it takes so much mental energy to focus on *what* you're saying, it's hard for most people to artificially raise their activity levels. Hence, Pentland's claim that activity is an honest signal. He's found that in speed-dating, the measurable activity level of the woman is the strongest predictor of whether or not she'll give out her phone number and contact information. Similarly, testing the theory at a conference, Pentland found that activity level was the best predictor of whether or not people shared contact information.

Here's the problem. It's hard to consciously increase your activity level. It's not impossible, but it's difficult to do gracefully and smoothly and still attend to the conversation.

The good news is that there's an important piece that Pentland's measure leaves out in this instance: focus. When we're focused on a conversation, a person, or a topic, we can raise our interest without artificially having to increase our activity.

So focusing emotionally before an important conversation, negotiation, meeting, or speech will help you raise your activity level, focus, and likelihood of engaging the people around you successfully. As I discussed in chapter 2, emotional focus also helps to bring charisma into the picture. It's not an honest signal that Pentland can measure, but it's essential for leadership in a distracted age. Focusing on the task at hand when you're in that conversation, negotiation, meeting, or speech will help as well, and keep you sharp in the game.

If you're a public speaker, you'll also need to do some rehearsal and preparation to tailor your activity to your setting. I'll explain more about this in the field notes at the end of the chapter. But in most smaller-scale conversations, you'll be able to increase your activity to an appropriate level if you focus emotionally beforehand and focus your presence in the moment itself.

When to Be Consistent? Not Always

The final honest signal is consistency. It's also perhaps the most surprising. Pentland's findings are fascinating. It turns out that it makes a difference as to whether you're pitching or listening. If you're a business executive pitching a business plan, for instance, then the more consistent the better. Similarly, you'll do better in salary negotiations if you're consistent. What consistency signals is determination, so people are more likely to give you what you're asking for if you're consistent.

But if you're engaged in listening, say, to a potential customer, then the opposite of consistency is more successful. That is, you want to show more variation in your manner at different times, because this signals openness to the other person. Variation means you're a better listener, and that increases the odds that you'll close the deal because people like to be listened to.

Why does consistency work in some situations and not others? Because we show inconsistency when we get new data, or information, that throws us off our prepared track. So when you're pitching to a venture capital group, for example, and get rattled by a question that one of your interlocutors asks, you'll decrease the chances of getting funding. The panel will unconsciously get the message that you're not prepared or not fully in control, and it will act accordingly.

On the other hand, if a client asks us a question that makes us reconsider some basic attitude or idea and we display inconsistency, the client feels listened to—and prefers that feeling.

Perhaps the clearest way to put it is to note that when you're looking for support, it's best to be consistent. But when you're trying to demonstrate openness to the other party, it's best to mix up your delivery.

How Emotional Should You Get in Public?

Showing genuine emotion by tearing up is another type of honest signal; it's not one of the four core areas, but if you do shed any tears, it will certainly capture your audience's attention. And the rules for emoting have changed.

A generation ago it was easy: public figures didn't cry in front of the cameras or in any sort of public setting. When Ed Muskie cried on the 1972 campaign trail, his candidacy more or less collapsed afterward. He was widely deemed too emotional to be president. Fast forward to 2008, and candidate Hillary Clinton's near-crying moment in January in New Hampshire. That episode was said by some to be a calculated effort to make her appear more human, whereas others said it was a genuine moment that made her appear more human. Finally, in the present day, we have Speaker of the House John Boehner, whose tendency to cry easily and frequently in public has gotten some press attention.

What's the right emotional tenor a leader should strike? Why do we make such a fuss about tears and other emotional outbursts? What does an emotional outburst say about the public figure in question? Here are a few rules for emotional behavior in public:

- *What's appropriate changes constantly; part of the test of a modern public figure is how well he or she reads the situation.* The reason the public reacted so strongly to Muskie's possible tears was that tears were out of the normal range of behavior for politicians of the day. The issue is not really one of emotion per se, but how well the public figure reads the situation and reacts. It's a test, in this sense, of emotional intelligence. If you push the envelope too far, you'll get a strong public reaction, either good or bad—or more likely both at once.

- *Emotional outbursts are hot TV; they will get covered.* There's no hiding if the cameras are rolling at the same time as the tears. TV is a cool medium, and it craves hot emotions. In other words, we love to watch people get angry, sad, happy, or whatever. As long as it's emotional and extreme, it will play well on TV and get lots of coverage.

- *When the emotion runs counter to the dominant story about you, it will make news.* Hillary Clinton's slight choking up on the campaign trail was big news because the dominant story about her was that she was a controlled, unemotional campaigner. There was a gender-based narrative about her as well: was she being tough in order to put questions to rest about her ability to dominate on the world stage because she is a woman? The tears might have been calculated, or they might have been real, but either way they were news because of the perception of Clinton's character. Did the tears support or undercut the narrative? That was the argument.

- *An established public figure can push the boundaries of currently acceptable behavior.* Boehner's teary speeches have become commonplace; he has pushed the boundaries of what is acceptable in a public emotional outburst. After a few stories, the press moved on to other things, because it absorbed this story into the main Boehner narrative. In other words, because Boehner is already well known on the American national stage and his story well established, his crying jags only add a plot point; they don't really undercut the main story.

- *Even as the emotional boundaries change, what stays the same is the importance of tact.* We expect some emotional intelligence from our leaders and some strength. Thus, restrained emotions will always play better than full-bore outbursts. The issue is that emotions are charismatic; we pay attention to and ultimately respect leaders who show anger, compassion, excitement, and the rest of the range of human emotions at the appropriate moment and at the appropriate pitch. The world has become far more accepting of public emotions in general, but we still expect our leaders to be tactful about them.

How to Send Honest Signals through Cyberspace

Here's another way our sense of what's normal is changing. The realities of twenty-first-century work life, especially post-2008, mean many of us have more virtual meetings than face-to-face ones. That represents a huge shift in organizational life in less than a generation. Of course, the purveyors of the high-tech equipment that makes these meetings possible tout the benefits—efficiency, speed, savings on travel, and so on. These are undeniable.

But what are the problems with this sea change in human behavior? I can see five major issues. As we've discussed, our unconscious minds handle the chore of sensing other people's attitudes and intents from body language. And because the way the brain remembers things is to attach emotion to them, if there's no intent or emotion, we don't remember much.

- *The first big problem with virtual communication is that it's very hard to remember anything* we hear in this way without that second stream of information our unconscious mind constantly feeds us about intent and emotion. Most of that second stream comes through body language, and most of that is cut out over the phone, so instantly our minds are not fully engaged, we can't read the emotional subtext very well, and we therefore can't remember much of what we hear.

- *The second big problem is related to the first. Attention spans are getting shorter.* Some recent research by John Medina suggests it may be as short as ten minutes. But habit dictates that meetings are usually scheduled in hour-long segments, some even longer. So our meetings, especially virtual ones, are outstripping our attention spans.

- *The third big problem is that you don't have the social cues* that indicate when your audience is puzzled, lost, interested, or bored; little of that gets through. A good meeting chairperson will constantly sense the atmosphere in the room and react accordingly—in a face-to-face meeting. That's impossible in a virtual meeting.

- *The fourth big problem follows from this one; misunderstandings easily develop* when social cues are absent. We've all experienced the mess you can make with one misinterpreted email, where somebody imagines a tone that you didn't mean. The same thing can happen in an audio conference. For example, does the silence in response to what you've just said mean everyone's in rapt agreement, or everyone's tuned out— or people are on mute so that they can have a party?

- *The last big problem that develops out of virtual meetings is that the bonding that naturally happens* when people meet face-to-face and size each other up, find mutual interests, and fall in love is lacking. As a result, commitment—trust—is fragile.

What can you do to put the life back into that sometime blessing, sometime curse of the modern world, virtual meetings?

- *Accept the less-than-perfect nature of virtual meetings.* Don't try to make virtual meetings into something they're not or try to make them carry freight they can't. Do the less important things via virtual meetings whenever possible. Save the emotional stuff for face-to-face meetings, because it's emotions and attitudes that are conveyed mostly via body language.

- *Have regular face-to-face meetings to reinvigorate the team.* If you're kicking off something important or celebrating a big win, or you have significant issues, bite the meeting bullet and bring everyone together. Trying to solve disagreements or rev people up via a digital phone line is pure folly. Our emotional investment in a phone call is simply less than in a face-to-face meeting, and the lack of visual and tonal information makes it much harder to get key messages across.

- *Never go longer than ten minutes without some kind of break.* Medina's evidence suggests that attention spans may be about ten minutes; our attention spans are certainly no longer on a phone, so plan your meeting in ten-minute segments and take breaks in between. The breaks will allow people to reengage. You can either stop the meeting entirely or just urge everyone to get up and stretch. People don't need a long break, just a chance for a quick change of pace.

- *Get regular group input.* What most people do during long phone meetings is put the phone on mute and take care of other chores while half-listening. You can keep the group involved by going around the phones asking for input. In a face-to-face meeting, you're able to tell how people are doing by monitoring their body language. In a virtual meeting, you need to stop regularly to take everyone's temperature. And I do mean everyone. Go right down the list, asking each locale or person for input.

- *Identify your emotions verbally.* Lacking visual cues, we have a very hard time reading other people's feelings, so make yours clear verbally and train other people on the call to do the same. Say, "I'm excited about everything we're accomplishing!" Or, "Bob, I'm concerned that you don't seem confident in the 3Q numbers. How are you really feeling about them?" You've got to put back in what the phone lines are removing.

- *Use video to bring the group together.* Face-to-face meetings allow a group to share emotions easily. That keeps them together and feeling connected.

That's much harder to do in a virtual meeting. So do the small talk—but make it video small talk. Get the group to send each other thirty-second or one-minute clips of what they're up to or what the weather's like where they are. Something personal really adds a sense of connection back to the group. Put some of that money you're saving on travel to good technological use.

Virtual meetings may never replace the need for humans to exchange emotional and unconscious nonverbal information through face-to-face exchanges, but they can make do for all but the most important purposes.

I wonder if something basic is changing in the way we form relationships. Will the next generations be able to invest in online connections the same way that everyone now invests in "real" face-to-face relationships?

Think for a moment about the nature of trust in the virtual world. It's much more fragile, though perhaps easier to establish initially. But the big difference comes when something threatens the trust.

In face-to-face relationships where there is trust, one party may do something to screw up, causing friction, anger, and even a bit of mistrust to creep in. But if the connection is strong enough, the issue will get thrashed out, the perpetrator will apologize, and trust will be restored. Indeed, once restored, the trust may be stronger than ever.

How different it is in the virtual world. Once trust is threatened, it's instantly broken, and it's virtually impossible to reestablish it. People simply move on. Since trust was more fragile in the first place, it shatters with very little provocation.

If most of your relationships are virtual, the fragility of those relationships may make you less able to get through the bumps and shocks that every (face-to-face) relationship naturally endures. If you take the pattern of commitment from the virtual world, your understanding of the meaning of relationship will be attenuated and weak.

On the other hand, if you can learn to master Pentland's honest signals, you'll radiate charisma—all the more power-fully because so many of our relationships are so fractured by our attempts to interact like disembodied brains instead of like the social animals we really are.

You can master these honest signals of social interaction with preparation, emotional focus, and presence. And now you know how to land that next job, that date, or that $40 million in funding. Dominate the proceedings, within tactful and appropriate limits. Establish harmony, trust, and connection with your mirroring body language and then lead the room, getting others to mirror you. Show a high level of engagement throughout the proceedings. And be consistent; don't let any-thing throw you. Sound like a tall order? It is if you try to wing it. But with preparation of spoken content, body language, and your underlying emotions, there's no reason why you can't be a winner nearly every time.

FIELD NOTES

Sending Honest Signals from the Stage

When you speak in public, there's a lot to do: you have to stand straight, act energetic, focus on the audience, remember your speech, keep your finger out of your ear, and so on. What are the main points to pay attention to?

You need to know your speech cold or you won't be able to do anything but struggle through. The ability to do more than survive depends on knowing the speech so well that you have some extra RAM to devote to all the other things you and the audience are supposed to be doing.

If you do know your speech, then the first place to put your focus is on you. Is your body language consistent with your message? In other words, if you're asking the assembled multitudes to work harder, stay later, and bring in more customers in order to meet a stretch goal for the third quarter, then do you look like someone who is already doing that? How is your posture? Is it straight and heart-oriented? If you're slouching, don't expect those in the audience to respond to your plea. You don't look as if you're ready to work, so why should they?

Then think about your body language in relation to the people in the audience. Are you looking at them or, more specifically, selected individuals within the audience in about thirty-second bursts? Is your face animated, energetic, and interested? Once again, if you're not having a fabulous time and showing it, don't expect the audience to respond.

Get Ready to Work the Room

One of the great questions for regular public speakers is, when I get there what will the room look like? Few of the places we speak have great sight lines, perfect acoustics, and comfortable seating for the audience. We're usually working with less-than-prime conditions. So it helps to be ready for most of the possibilities. In other words, be ready to answer the question, *how will I use this room to my advantage and work the crowd?* with minimal stress and uncertainty.

If you're thinking, *I just stand behind the podium, look down for my notes, and fire away, and let the audience take care of itself*, then you don't have much to worry about. Your audience may well fall asleep, but why should that concern you?

Choreograph Your Talk

If you want to actually reach your audience and change the world by moving them to action, then you're going to need to choreograph your talk.

Here's why. As I've said, every face-to-face communication is two conversations—the content and the body language. Most speakers spend a lot of time thinking about content and very little thinking about body language. As a result, most speakers' two conversations are not aligned, and they are not effective communicators. For example, a common trap that speakers fall into stems from their use of PowerPoint. They cue up a slide, facing their computer, half-turned from the audience, looking at the screen to see that the next slide is in fact the one they're expecting. Then, they may turn back to the audience to explain the slide.

But just before they finish that explanation, they turn back to the computer, because their mind is racing ahead of their mouths, and they want to cue up the next slide.

Beware the Body Language Message

When someone turns away from us, the body language message is, *you're not important, or, what I'm saying is not important,* or, *I'm finished with you.* That's the message that conflicts with the end of the explanation of the slide. I call it the PowerPoint triangle of death, because the speaker tends to stand midway between screen and computer, moving slightly toward one or the other, forming a triangle of body language that is signaling disinterest and disconnection to the audience.

How to Increase the Audience's Interest

The good news is that focusing on the talk at hand and carefully choreographing your talk will prevent this weak message from coming through to your audience.

Every time you move toward the audience, its interest level is raised. Every time you move away from the audience, the audience cools down. An audience unconsciously monitors the space between it and the speaker. More than twelve feet is public space, and our unconscious minds are not strongly engaged. If the speaker comes within twelve feet, but not as close as four feet, that's social space, and the audience starts to pay attention. Less than four feet, and the people in the audience are in personal space and suddenly wide awake and fully engaged.

So your goal is to move into that personal space (but not closer than one-and-a-half feet, because that's intimate space and you're not allowed in there, unless with a close friend or family member). That's where your audience will be paying attention most powerfully.

Use Your Audience's Mirror Neurons

But wait, you say, how can I get into the personal space of an audience of five hundred people? You can't, of course, but here's where a property of the human mind comes into play. As I've indicated earlier, we have mirror neurons in our brains whose sole purpose is to fire away when we see someone nearby experiencing an emotion. So if we see the speaker coming toward another audience member, our interest is piqued in the same way as if the speaker were moving toward us.

The effect diminishes over space and large numbers of people, so you need to work the crowd as much as you can, but you need to get into the personal space of only a few people in the audience for everyone to feel connected with you.

Do you begin to get the choreography that is involved in making a speech? You want to move toward select members of the audience when you're making a point and then only move away when you've finished the point and are ready to go to the next one.

How does this dance work in practice? You want to first study your speech to find the high points. What are the three to six most important moments in the speech? Those are the points when you want to be in the personal space of a selected audience member.

Now, in order to balance your approach to the audience, divide it up into sections in your mind. Begin your speech standing stage center, where everyone can see you. After the first few minutes, then begin to move to stage right and find an audience member on your right hand who can represent that section of the audience. Make your point to that person. Then, a few minutes later, move to stage left. Repeat. Move back to stage center. And so on. Work the room in rotation, without making it look mechanical. Finish your speech back at stage center.

Now consider some of the variations involved in some typical room layouts.

The U-Shape

My favorite room layout by far is the *U*. You can begin your speech in the center, at the top of the *U*, and work the audience easily up and down the sides. You're never far from anyone, and everyone feels connected. Some *U*'s are several rows deep; for those you may want to walk up—once or twice only—into the second row, depending on how hard it is to navigate. But never stay deep in an audience for a long time, because some people will only see your back facing them, and that's not good for the reasons I've already outlined.

Classroom Style

The success of a classroom style layout depends on how many aisles there are. If there's at least one, you can work the aisle to get deep into the rows at least once or twice. If there's no aisle, then the studies show that you'll only connect with people who are in an inverse triangle in relation to the front. The base of the triangle is the front row, and the tip is at the back center. It's why goodie-goodies sit at the front of the classroom, and hooligans sit at the back. The former want to connect with teacher, and the latter do not.

Auditorium Style

Auditorium-style layouts give you lots of opportunities to work the aisles, provided that they're accessible and you don't have to leap over obstructions or climb down dimly lit stairs to get to them. When you study the hall beforehand, decide on your strategy. If it's too difficult to get into the audience, then work the stage. The audience will interpret your efforts as attempting to get to them, and that's second best. Once again, don't spend too long deep in the aisles, because people can only turn with difficulty in auditorium-style seating.

Rounds

Rounds are perhaps the worst sort of settings, because it's very hard to work the audience when it's spread all over and facing in different directions. Yet it's a style you will see in hotels across the known universe. Meeting planners love rounds, because they can set the tables and put interesting centerpieces on them, they can feed the audience, and so on. But rounds are tough on speakers.

You still need to work the audience; in fact, you need to work harder. Try to negotiate with the meeting planner to have the rounds only half-filled, facing the front, so at least half the audience won't have its back turned toward you. Keep the house lights turned up if possible, and consider beginning your talk in the back of the room in order to get closer to the people there. Then move to the front and work the center, left, and right, going into the second set of rounds once or twice.

Rectangular Breakout Rooms

These rooms are where audiences go to die. They're long, the acoustics are typically awful, and the ceilings are low. People in the audience feel as if they're in a shoebox and tend to sit near the back so that they can make surreptitious exits halfway through. In these rooms, ask the audience to move forward to the front rows, pleading acoustics, and work the front, left, and right sides. If there's a center row, use that to get deep into the shoebox once during the talk in order to revivify the audience in the back.

Good choreography is the quickest way to raise your speaking a level from mediocre, everyday, and average, to memorable and world changing. Practice making your moves while talking and smiling at the same time. You'll be richly rewarded with positive audience feedback. Audiences crave a connection with their speakers, and this is the best way to give it to them.

CHAPTER SUMMARY

- MIT researchers have determined four patterns of behavior that predict success or failure in certain key human interactions: influence, mimicry, activity, and consistency. These are the so-called "honest signals."

- You can increase your success as a leader or as a salesperson, or pitching to a venture capitalist and so on, by consciously using each of the patterns of behavior to ensure that you project power and control in a given situation.

- To increase your influence, increase positional power, emotion, or expertise, or control the give-and-take tempo of the conversation.

- To increase your mimicry, consciously copy others; then lead them.

- To increase your activity, focus more intently on the conversation, meeting, or presentation.

- Increase your consistency to gain support; decrease it to show openness.

- The virtual nature of our world makes it harder to project honest signals.

CHAPTER SIX

Using Your Intuition Effectively

What Your Gut Is Really Saying— and How to Leverage It

I'll talk in this chapter about the role of intuition—your unconscious life—in guiding and shaping how you experience stress, manage your career, and strive to reach your full potential. Western science is only just beginning to discover what the role of the gut is in our emotional and intellectual lives, but some early clues can help get you started on turning into a leader, using the power of your unconscious mind to propel you ahead in life.

A Mixed Report Card

Western science, despite all the progress it has made in eighty years since antibiotics were discovered, has a few mysteries left to plumb. One of them is, what is the true role of the unconscious mind, the gut, or intuition in our mental lives? The way I've phrased the question suggests the beginning of an answer: what we colloquially call our gut—the place we go when we want to make a decision, a bet, or a guess, without much intellectual support, which most people would agree is roughly equivalent to what we mean by our intuition—is actually our unconscious mind at work.

But, of course, even as we redefine the problem, we make it bigger, because our understanding of what we mean by "unconscious mind" is growing all the time. I'll discuss more of that in a moment.

First, I should pause here to acknowledge that we're at the frontiers of Western scientific understanding, and some of the contents of this chapter may well make you uncomfortable. If you're the sort of person who squirms during a discussion of New Age ideas like mind control, then be warned. This chapter is all about mind control. What I'm going to do is put you in charge of that part of your mental life that you've hitherto thought was out of (conscious) reach: intuition. If you think that's crazy, then skip this chapter and go right to chapter 7, which is all about storytelling, still mind control, but for which there's a good deal of new scientific evidence, not to mention ancient wisdom.

OK, so let's get started.

Power Cue 6: Is your unconscious mind holding you back or propelling you forward?

You've begun the process of focusing and controlling your emotions for important conversations, meetings, negotiations, presentations, and so on. You've learned to harness the power of your unconscious mind to read other people reliably and quickly. You've learned how to increase the leadership potential of your voice. And you understand the so-called honest signals that guide social interactions and have learned how to control those in order to be successful.

You've taken inventory of your body language, which will have given you your first insights into the unconscious emotions, intents, and attitudes that lie behind that nonverbal communication, especially the habitual postures and gestures of your body. These have developed over time and represent characteristic ways you respond to the world. They are representative of how you think and feel about both good and bad events, stress and joy, opportunities and disasters.

As such, they're a palimpsest of all your accumulated reactions, decisions, fears, and joys. In a very real sense, your personal history is written in your body and its literal, physical attitude toward the world.

Is your body defiant, or do you stand like a victim? Do you dominate the space or take up as little as possible? Are you a leader or a second in command? Do you effortlessly lead a team to get things done, or do you spend huge amounts of time keeping score of all the little ups and downs you encounter along the way, like a spider weaving memories into her web? All of this shows up in your body, especially as it ages.

That presentation to the world becomes more and more unmistakably you, but it also, naturally enough, comes to limit the possibilities as time goes on.

That's potentially damaging enough. But when you reflect that most of those attitudes, intents, emotions, and desires that come to shape your body's typical response to the world are *unconscious* and shaped by your unconscious memories, then you start to see why it's so important that you understand what's going on.

Get to Know Your Gut

It's time you got to know your gut; that's the sixth step in this process of mastering your unconscious relationship with the world. There's a lot of folk wisdom about the gut, and how you should trust it sometimes and be smarter than it at other times, but the reality is far more complicated and surprising.

Let's talk about your physical gut first. We have something like 100 million neurons in our gut. It's a little brain, approximately as big as a cat's. It is the only part of our bodies not completely stage-managed by the big brain in our heads. It's capable of autonomous action, and that's a good thing, because it takes care of the all-important task of converting food into the energy that keeps our systems going. Further, it defends our bodies against poison, bad food, and your Aunt Millie's stew. The question is, what else does it do?

Researchers are just beginning to puzzle out the answer to that question. Heribert Watzke, the author of "The Brain in Your Gut," likes to say, "There sleeps a little cat," about the second brain, because it's about as powerful as a cat's brain.[1] He goes on to say, "Our gut has a full-fledged brain." That little, but full-fledged, cat-sized brain is connected—and this is the important part—to the emotional or limbic system of the big brain. Its chores include chemical and mechanical sensing of food, control of muscle movements like your gag reflex, as well as the hormones and enzymes that actually digest your food. The little brain produces hunger and satiation signals that the big brain happily ignores as you go back for that second helping of stuffing or eat that bowl of ice cream you know you're going to be wearing on your hips tomorrow. As far as we know now in Western science, the little brain has as its goals, as Watzke says, "the digestion and defense of your body."

But there's more going on than that.

The feedback between the two brains—or more specifically among the big brain, little brain, unconscious mind, and conscious mind—works both ways. When we say we have "butterflies" in our stomach, what we're talking about is the emotional connection between the big brain, its unconscious part, and the little brain. The signals can originate in either place and send terror racing up the vagus nerve from the gut to the unconscious mind, and after that to the conscious mind.

The result is that we can feel fear, for example, before we know it (consciously) or its source. Messages from the gut create emotion, and emotions in the big brain give us indigestion or worse.

So the two brains communicate in a variety of ways that we're still determining in Western science. Chinese medicine has connected the two brains for centuries via *chi*, and current research into the functioning of the vagus nerve suggests that it may be one of the prime pathways of communication between the two brains.

Your *Chi* May Be Telling You Something

Michael Gershon, author of *The Second Brain*, goes even further. He says, "What the gut does is extremely complicated. It manages digestion, it manages absorption, and it protects you from invasion. Because after all each of us is a hollow human being. The lining of the gut is the surface that separates the outside world from your body." It's the barrier between things that will help you and things that will hurt you. More than that, and this is important, Gershon says, "It's the only part of the body that has independence" from the big brain.[2]

In effect, Gershon notes, "Evolution decided it works more efficiently to have a set of microprocessors within the gut itself. The brain is like an important CEO who doesn't like to micromanage." OK, so why would we humans end up, evolutionarily speaking, as more of an assemblage than a unit, and what does that mean for how well we function?

Which brings us to serotonin. By now, everyone's familiar with that delightful chemical, the one that makes your brain and, therefore you, happy. But it turns out that making life worthwhile is only one tiny aspect of what serotonin does. Only 2 percent of all the serotonin in the body is to be found in your head, keeping you smiling and helping regulate things like aging, learning, and memory.

The rest of it is in your gut, making you sick. Gershon explains, "It can trigger responses in the gut that are unpleasant. It may be released when the gut is threatened with infection and cause diarrhea or inflammation as it tries to protect against infection. You can think of it as a Roman legion. They went to battle with spears and swords; that's like the serotonin in the lining of the gut, and they went to battle with shields, in this case represented by serotonin in your gut's nerve cells. This legion of serotonin fights off infection and foreign invaders. Gershon continues, "Some of the signals that don't come to consciousness are good and might improve mood. The cross talk between the gut and the brain is important. So maybe information from the gut can help keep the brain on the even keel." But also, "The gut has a very profound ability to disturb the brain."

So serotonin, thanks to the differing functions of various parts of the human body, is a two-edged sword, like the ones those Roman legions wielded. It is just like adrenaline, which both energizes and terrifies us, enabling us to do our best, but also making us devilishly uncomfortable at the same time. And, if we can't control it, that adrenaline in the end undermines us and leads us to do stupid things in front of large audiences. This is all because of the double-edged nature of the way humans respond to the environment and, particularly, stress in the environment.

The little brain in your gut can communicate misery or harmony to the big brain in your head and vice versa. So the old way of thinking, that it's your job to control your thoughts to help with nerves, say, when you're about to perform in an important meeting or presentation, is too simplistic. Any sort of intervention has to figure out how to send signals in both directions.

How Your Body Sabotages You at the Wrong Times

What we're learning is that the human body is an assemblage of systems that have a surprising degree of autonomy from one another, and that are all busy managing various aspects of your mental and physical lives. Nonetheless, they do communicate with one another, and that's why the human assemblage works pretty well most of the time.

Except when we're trying to do something difficult, like start a new job demanding all sorts of skills and abilities that we've only partly tried out before. Or we're standing in front of an audience getting ready to give a speech to a group of concerned stakeholders in our organization. Or we're trying to persuade the executive team to go in a new, relatively untried direction, betting the company on the hope of success. Or, perhaps, we're in the middle of a job interview for a position we've been scheming to get for several years, one that would allow us to try out the vision we have for the future of our industry.

In those instances, the polyglot nature of our bodies betrays us as often as it propels us to victory. The little brain may disable us by sending messages of abject terror shooting up to our big brains, causing embarrassing physical symptoms that become impossible for us—and the others in the room—to ignore. Or the big brain may make a mess of things by going blank at a key moment, causing us to fail to close the deal or wow the crowd when the chance comes.

The bottom line is that if you're only working on your brain to send signals down to your gut, you're doing less than half the job necessary for success. And that perhaps is why most efforts to control nerves in that way are so ineffectual.

Instead, you want to start a new, more sophisticated dialogue, not just between brain and body, but between big brain, unconscious and conscious brains, little brain, and body. You want to ensure that your gut is supporting your big brain and body, and the other way around. You want to get all the systems working together to ensure that you're operating at peak efficiency at those moments when you need to be at the top of your game.

Your Unconscious Mind Is a Mishmash

At the moment, what's going on? The dialogue you currently have is mostly unmanaged and is a collection of old thoughts, both conscious and unconscious (mostly unconscious) fears, compulsive behavior, things that worked well once upon a time, and so on. It's a mishmash.

To make matters worse, it's an unconscious mishmash. Things your parents told you in moments of fatigue and pique, things that you've forgotten, shape your thinking along with lessons your body has learned about all the stimuli it has received since the womb. Things you've heard, stupid jokes your friends told you when you were eight, movies you've seen, books you've read, memories of being lost in the dunes during that summer on Nantucket, and so on, all jumble together in your unconscious mind, random data that it has assembled from everything that it has seen, heard, smelled, tasted, and felt.

The unconscious brain apparently never forgets. Everything it has experienced is set somewhere in the 100 billion or so cells that make up our vast internal universe. But the way the mind works is that things that are repeated are strengthened, making stronger and more numerous synapses, so that the memory becomes more and more important to our overall patterns of thinking. We attach emotions to events to create memories. The more intense and more frequent an event is—as it strikes us—the more it looms large in our mental attic.

So, for example, if your brain links together the experience of choosing up sides in sports encounters in grade school with your popularity in later years, the social dynamics of your relationships with your colleagues at work, and your divorce, you may have a significant and largely unconscious set of beliefs about your ability to manage a team that kick into place when you get that new promotion. You may find yourself self-sabotaging without knowing why.

Thanks to the usual unavailability of the unconscious sources of most of our attitudes and beliefs, we may have very strongly held feelings that hold us back without knowing the reason. If we knew the reason, we might be surprised or even appalled.

The reality is that your conscious mind is beset by essentially random directives from your unconscious mind, some of which help you succeed in your larger purposes in life and most of which don't.[3]

Beware Lack of Control

When you're not in control of those random directives from your unconscious mind, you risk ineffectiveness. I once saw the magic act of Penn and Teller, two accomplished magicians. Penn is the talkative one, and Teller is largely silent. Penn keeps up a running commentary designed to distract and bemuse the audience while they both perform the magic tricks.

I was astonished to see that the talkative one, Penn, had a bad case of "happy feet." He had so much energy that he was wandering all over the stage randomly while chattering away. The random movement of his feet was his method of discharging the adrenaline-induced energy that his body was generating.

The result was so distracting, though, that I found myself unable to attend to his patter or even the magic tricks with any real pleasure. Nonetheless, he managed to hold his audience reasonably well until he and Teller performed an unpleasant trick that involved apparently putting a live rabbit through a wood chipper. He lost his audience then and never got it back, making it clear that the bond was weak from the start, partly because of those irritating happy feet. Had he bonded strongly with the audience from the start, the relationship would have survived the murder of rabbits.

It's impossible to believe that a successful professional like Penn was not aware of his motion around the stage. I'm forced to conclude that he was simply unable to control it, and that lack of control was fatal for the success of the show.

He was even heckled by one or two audience members and approached by at least one after the show, who gave him a lecture on the mistreatment of animals. Because he had not related effectively to the audience, thus building trust, when the moment of truth came, the audience didn't trust him.

Would an Athlete Train This Way?

When you don't bring your unconscious mind under control, you let the little cat-sized brain in your gut run the show. You let patterns and experiences from your past dictate your action in the present. It's as if an athlete training for a big race found herself occasionally running sideways or flailing her arms in random ways, just because she did that once as a kid to avoid something scary. If you're just running in a friendly competition, your occasionally bizarre performance won't matter much. But if you suddenly find yourself in the Olympics, the subtleties matter enormously. In that rare circle where hundredths of a second make the difference between the winning platform and a footnote, everything matters, especially your unconscious mind.

The same is true in leadership. You can get away with a lot when the stakes are low. But as you rise through the ranks, your hostility toward certain kinds of people, your tendency to procrastinate, your idea that people should be able to read your mind, or any one of a thousand other counterproductive beliefs I've seen managers act on will start to damage your ability to get the job done.

The higher up you go, the more certain self-destructive behaviors matter, and the more they'll be held against you. Plenty of people, alas, have affairs, because they're narcissists whose egos need constant feeding, but when you're running for president, it makes the news. Similarly, the bigger the P&L you manage, any less-than-optimal behavior patterns are more subject to scrutiny.

What are the options open to you if you discover that your 360-degree evaluation points out some uncomfortable truths you've been suppressing for too long? You can try to change your behavior, you can get therapy and hope that will change your behavior, or you can deny that there's any problem and keep doing the same things with the same people and hope for different results.

Just changing behavior is difficult, and you're liable to relapse. Therapy is time consuming, expensive, and the results are mixed. And denial doesn't work unless you're lucky for the rest of your life.

There's an Alternative to Therapy

There is another way. The good news is that you can take charge of all your mental systems and learn to manage your unconscious mind as well as the mind in your gut and your conscious mind. It takes some time, but it will allow you to shed a good deal of the misinformation sloshing around in your head and body currently and become a better-focused human dynamo capable of sustained achievement. Athletes have been harnessing a little bit of the power of their unconscious minds by practicing mental imaging of their races and games for many years. The results are extraordinary, beginning with the gold medal counts the Soviets achieved back in the era of the Cold War and spreading around the world in subsequent years.[4]

Now it's time for the rest of us to get with the program, clean up our mental attics, and start living up to our true potential. This three-step process takes about three to four weeks to show results at first, if you really push yourself, and up to three months, if you're slower. After that, all it takes is maintenance.

The process begins with identifying the irrational fears, beliefs, and habits that are getting in the way of your performance in a particular area. Then, you develop the new dialogues that you need to replace the old fixations. Finally, you implement the new thinking. I'll describe each step in more detail later in the chapter.

How Useful Is That Unconscious Mind Really?

I know what you're thinking. Most of us have some sense that intuition is good for some things and not so good for others. We look down on—even pity—the person who merely relies on gut feel, say, for large financial bets or important decisions. Yet we've all heard stories of times when the gut has prevailed and the answer turned out to be the right one. How can the unconscious mind help with something as deeply held, complex, and obscured in the mists of time as neurotic fears?

Here, most of the folk wisdom we've learned about the unconscious is useless, because it doesn't really get to the heart of the problem: how can you start sending out "winning" messages instead of "losing" ones with just your voice and body?

Try the following thought experiment. Put yourself in your best suit. Put yourself in an office, at 8:30 a.m., waiting for the biggest day of your career to date. You've got a chance to change your industry. A group of CEOs are meeting to discuss some standards for the things your industry produces, standards that will save consumers huge amounts of confusion and companies huge amounts of money. But there's a lot of resistance to your ideas in that group of CEOs, because they're fiercely competitive, suspicious of one another, and reluctant to cooperate. How comfortable are you walking into that room full of CEOs and taking charge of the meeting? Are you comfortable, a little nervous, quite nervous, especially at first, or terrified?

Most people would come down on the "a little nervous" to "quite nervous, especially at first," part of the scale, depending on the importance of the meeting to the overall program. But if you're anywhere on that scale besides "comfortable," you've got work to do. Because the truth is that while adrenaline has its uses, and it shares many characteristics with fear, it is not the same thing. The two often get conflated in our minds, because the physical symptoms are so similar. But they don't have to be.

I used to ask my public speaking students at Princeton at the beginning of term how many of them got nervous before making a speech. Virtually all of them raised their hands. Then I would ask how they knew they were nervous. Now, this was a bit of an oddball question, because they hadn't thought about their nerves in this way before, but after a little head scratching, these smart folks would come up with a credible list of physical symptoms that indicated to them that they were nervous. Their hearts beat fast, their palms got sweaty, their minds raced, their faces flushed, they got weak at the knees, and so on.

Then I would say to the students, "Forget public speaking for a moment and listen to this list." I would repeat the symptoms they had just relayed to me and ask, "What's about to happen?"

Inevitably, some smart-aleck student would get a big laugh from the roomful of twenty-one-year-olds by saying, "You're about to have sex!"

The point, which they never failed to make, is that those physical symptoms which you interpret as terribly uncomfortable when you're about to give a speech get a completely different, and far more pleasurable, interpretation when you're looking forward to something else.

For many students, it was an "aha" moment because it taught them that they could begin to discriminate amongst physical reactions, unconscious attitudes, and beliefs.

Like Those Princeton Students, You're Ready for the Cure

What we're going to focus on now is the unconscious work that you have to do to keep from giving up leadership automatically in those first few minutes of any conversation, meeting, negotiation, presentation, or high-stakes event, where the top dog gets sorted out from all the other dogs. The precise form of your fear will be different from everyone else's, but everyone has those fears, attitudes, and beliefs getting in the way of their leadership potential.

If you believe that you're not capable of taking charge, then you will almost certainly signal that to everyone else in the room, too. What you have to do is change that belief, because it lives most strongly in your unconscious.

First, Identify Your Fears

OK, let's start the cure. First, you need to identify whatever is holding you back. Let's take the example of public speaking, because it's such a common fear. (I'll talk more about how to conquer this common fear in the field notes at the end of this chapter.) Let's say that you've been promoted to vice president in your organization, and the position requires that you give regular speeches to a wide variety of stakeholders. You're going to have to speak about once a week to crowds of one hundred or more at a pop.

The problem is that the prospect terrifies you. You're OK talking to your team or your colleagues in small numbers on a regular basis, sitting around a table. You see those as less formal, more casual events, part of everyday work, not a *speech*. It's something about the idea of a *speech* that causes you to feel faint and have visions of cardiac arrest.

But what causes that reaction to giving a speech? Is it the impression you have that a speech is more formal? Is it that you're talking to strangers for the most part? Is it some idea that a *speech* operates under different rules, rules you never learned very well because you didn't pay close attention in that communications course in college? In fact, you failed it, and the shame lingers on.

You need to figure out as precisely as you can what the fear is, what the belief is that is holding you back. This is not an easy task. You have to probe your fear as you would probe an infected wound. It hurts. It's not pleasant. You won't want to go there. But go there you must. Figure it out. Be honest with yourself, look as deep as you can, and get as close to the bottom of it that you can.

Then state your fear as clearly as possible: "I get nervous when I have to speak to strangers because I'm afraid they're judging me like that popular clique of students did, snickering at me and making fun of me when I gave that stupid speech about bees in the sixth grade."

Once you've identified the fear as clearly as you can, let it sit for a day or two. Writing it down helps. Come back and visit it at least a couple of times over a twenty-four-hour period. See if it still hurts.

If you've followed the steps in this book, then you've already strengthened your connection to your unconscious mind considerably. You've gotten used to listening to it. Now, you need to listen very carefully to your unconscious mind and hear if it's telling you that this is the right fear. If it is, you'll know it. It will resonate with your unconscious mind.

Second, Develop the Antidote

Once you've got the fear clearly stated and you're satisfied that it's as close as you're going to get, then work on finding the countervailing positive statement. Perhaps it's this: "I get excited when I speak to strangers because it's a wonderful opportunity to make new friends and spread the word about my cause. It's fun!"

There are several key points to keep in mind. The unconscious isn't very good with negative thinking, so state everything in a positive way. Avoid negative words and negative phrasing. Don't say, "I don't get nervous when I speak to strangers," because your unconscious will hear "nervous" and that will reinforce the nervousness you already have. The neurons already in place will be reinforced. Instead say, "I get excited …"

Next, make sure you state the positive opposite emotion or attitude to your fear as precisely as possible. You're creating a smart bullet to target the fear, and you want to take it out precisely. So make the correspondence to your fear as exact as possible, but phrased as a positive alternative.

Finally, make it as simple as possible, but still comprising a full sentence with a subject and a verb. As you'll see when I discuss implementation, you're going to be intimately living with this sentence for quite a while, so simplicity is a virtue.

Write it down, let it sit for at least twenty-four hours, and come back to it a few times to check to make sure it still works. Imagine if this sentence were true. Would your issue go away?

Ask yourself that question, and let your unconscious mind answer it.

Once you're sure you've got your antidote, your mantra, you're ready for implementation.

Third, Change Your Beliefs, Change the World

I am not a believer in that mumbo-jumbo from *The Secret* that says if you just believe that a million dollars will manifest itself in your pocket, it will.[5] But I do think that if you believe that you are a follower, you will always be treated like one. Because you will stand, walk, and speak like a follower. If you believe that you're a leader, you'll get a chance to lead. Not because of magic, but because you'll send out unconscious signals that will tell the rest of the world what to think about you.

If you are nervous going into a meeting of powerful people, that's because you don't believe, at some level, that you belong there. The only way to take charge in that case is to change your belief, so that you don't telegraph to everyone else that you are not worthy of notice.

For the most part, we accept what other people tell us about themselves. We don't have time for the alternative. We especially accept what other people's unconscious minds telegraph about themselves to our unconscious minds, because we're not even aware that we have taken it on board.

So how do you do it? How do you turn yourself into a fearless, positive, neurosis-free go-getter? The implementation is quite simple, but it takes discipline and patience. Remember that you're replacing synapses that have been firing for a long time, perhaps years, with varying degrees of intensity, and you are now replacing those connections with new ones. Persistence and patience will replace old trauma, but it will take time.

So it's time to start a new dialogue with your unconscious, one that tells your unconscious that actually you are a confident public speaker ("I get excited when I speak to strangers because it's a wonderful opportunity to make new friends and spread the word about my cause. It's fun!"). Or perhaps one that tells your unconscious mind what a relaxed, easy-going, natural-born leader you are. Something like, "I'm comfortable wielding power, and I do it with ease." Or, one that expresses your natural ability to lead on the fly: "I naturally take charge of the room when I go into a meeting." Whatever fits you and your circumstances best and most specifically.

You're going to say this line to yourself every chance you get, but especially when you're falling asleep, waking up, or having doubts or worries about your leadership capacity. Most especially, you're going to say it when the old doubts, fears, and issues start themselves up in your mind. Every single time a negative thought creeps into your mind, it's time to state your positive alternative. Let the line become your mantra. Say it (to yourself) hundreds of times a day if necessary.

Do this for three weeks, and you'll find yourself becoming more authoritative, confident, or whatever it is you've worked on. In three months, you'll find that you are effortlessly facing new situations that would have slowed you down or paralyzed you in the past. How quickly you proceed will be determined by how often you say your mantra and how often you neutralize the negative thoughts as they come up.

Here are a few pointers. First, stay patient and calm. Don't argue with your unconscious. Just simply repeat your mantra every time a negative thought along those lines bubbles up into your conscious mind.

Second, don't forget to say your mantra with especial dedication, over and over again, when you're falling asleep or if you wake up in the middle of the night and have trouble getting back to sleep. It's now a great opportunity for you to make quick progress. Just keep repeating that mantra until you fall asleep, like counting sheep.

Third, keep doing it even though you won't see much happening at first. Changing fundamental attitudes like this takes time. Changing unconscious attitudes takes time. Changing fundamental unconscious attitudes takes the most time.

Stay patient, stay focused, stay calm, and keep talking to yourself. That's all you have to do. You're replacing a negative doom-loop thought process with a virtuous, positive one.

How and why does this work? You've developed your own attitudes toward yourself and what you're capable of through hundreds of significant moments in your life—when you were picked or not picked for the team, when someone teased you, or you won a game, when you were singled out for praise or blame, and on and on. Each of these moments begins to contribute to a self-image that coalesces around what you think you're capable of over the years.

You've hard-wired your unconscious mind to think about yourself in a certain way. Now, you're simply rewiring your mind. It's not difficult to do; it just takes persistence.

It's Not Magic; It's an Unconscious Dialogue

Next, there's the external validation. Let's say you're working on a leadership mantra. As soon as the mantra starts to work and you start to notch some wins, you'll start to get positive emotional reinforcement for what's happening. So each time you come up winning, you stand a little straighter, walk a little more confidently, look people in the eye with more authority. Most importantly, your brain begins to strengthen the positive neural connections and weaken the negative ones. You become what you tell yourself you are.

Or, there's the alternative. Each time you lose, the opposite happens. Eventually, either way, you define a pattern, and that's what you believe. Which would you rather have your unconscious mind reinforcing? Which would you rather be learning in every fiber of your being?

What happens is that your unconscious mind, which is faster and more powerful than your conscious mind, determines your emotional state. Those attitudes, intents, and emotions get expressed in your physical gestures. And those gestures are what other people read to figure you out. You get constant reinforcement from the people around you based on what you're emoting as to what's possible for you to achieve from your own mind.

When your mother told you to stand up straight and look people in the eye, she wasn't wrong. It's just that it's impossible to follow that advice, because within seconds your conscious mind will move on to something else, and your body will go back to the unconscious expression of your true feelings. You're stuck with the pattern you've developed over many years of experience.

The good news is that you can change the pattern. Now, you get to pick the pattern that you want. So make it one that helps you to succeed. If you do nothing, then you'll end up with the self-description that is the sum total of everything that's gone right and wrong in your life.

Don't leave it up to chance like that. Take charge of your inner leadership life. Tell yourself the story that you want to live. As you develop a new self-story, you'll find that people begin to react to you differently. With your new belief will come a new way of interacting with the world, and that's necessary groundwork for becoming a more powerful leader. Not through any magic, but because you are carving a new way through human relations. This work will set the stage for the essential work on the voice that will help you seal the deal with your leadership.

I've seen this process succeed over and over with clients as they begin to change the thousand little messages they send out every day to their family, friends, and colleagues that define who they are among their fellows. All it takes is positive self-talk, lots and lots of positive self-talk. Be patient. It takes time to talk yourself into a new way of being.

FIELD NOTES

Positive Self-Talk as Public Speaking Prep

When you stand up to speak in front of others, you're risking a great deal. You can fail to engage the crowd, you can make a fool of yourself, you can attempt too little or too much and miss the mark. While the risk is almost always greater in your own mind than it is in reality, it is a real risk nonetheless.

One of the universal constants in the public speaking world is fear. Most speakers have it, a few manage to avoid it, and some are crushed by it. Not long ago, I worked with a client with a fear of *opening* a speech. He was fine once he got going, but those first few minutes were debilitating. Whenever I give a speech myself, after taking about a month or so off for coaching, I find myself rusty and nervous just like everyone else.

That fear is what causes people to play it safe when they're preparing their presentations. Ironically, that's the most dangerous tack to take. Playing safe means you go for the dull rather than the emotional, the read rather than the conversational, and the preachy rather than the interactive. All of those choices feel safer and are liable to produce a less successful presentation. They are choices that close you off to your potential audiences rather than opening you up to them.

If you're preparing a presentation, go for openness. Risk big, rather than playing it safe. Then, when you're actually delivering, try to begin right away avoiding self-protection. Get over yourself and your nerves. Put your focus on the audience. Be open to the people in the audience. If you can manage that, they will carry you and give you back far more energy that you put out.

The irony is that the best way to protect yourself in public speaking is to give up any thought of self-protection at all. Here's how:

Redefine the fear as adrenaline and, therefore, a good thing. This method is my personal favorite, and it works pretty well if you stick to it doggedly. When we're faced with having to speak in front of a crowd—or the prospect of one—the adrenaline starts flowing. It's the well-known flight-or-fight syndrome that helps you get ready to do battle with ancient enemies. In addition to the annoying symptoms like dry mouth, shaky knees, or clammy palms, your brain works faster, you have more energy, and you look a little larger than life. That's all good. So focus on the good things that those symptoms are bringing you, and you'll start to think differently about those clammy palms.

Rehearse, rehearse, rehearse. Rehearse a lot. Rehearsal is the best way to deal with nerves, objectively speaking, because when you do something a lot, you get comfortable with it and thus are less likely to get frightened about it. Rehearsal has the added benefit of most likely making you better at the presentation, certainly better than if you wing it. You'll look more polished because your body will signal to the audience, "I've done this before; I'm cool."

Breathe deeply, from the belly. Breathe slowly and often. Breathing is good for you, your voice, and your composure. A slow, deep belly breath supported from the diaphragmatic muscles will start an autonomic relaxation response that nicely counteracts those feelings of terror, so start at the first sign of symptoms. Because those belly breaths will ground you, make sure you do them just before you get up to speak, while you're being introduced, for example.

Focus on the audience, not on yourself. The real insight at the core of successful public speaking is that it isn't about you, it's about the audience getting it (or you were never there, in some sense). So focus on the audience, let go of yourself, and have a great time. I think of this as the Zen insight into public speaking, and it is truly liberating if you can convince yourself of it.

Focus on an emotion that you want to convey to the audience. If you're the sort of speaker who starts riffing on all the things that might go wrong when you get nervous about speaking, then you're like most of us. The idea is to replace that doom loop with something more productive. For a host of reasons, replacing nervous mental chatter with a strong emotion is a great substitute. First, figure out what emotion is appropriate to the beginning of your speech. It might be anger, joy, excitement, whatever. Then, recall a time when you felt that emotion naturally and strongly. But don't just remember it; relive it. Recall what it smelled, tasted, looked, sounded, and felt like. Shut your eyes and put yourself there. With practice, this can become a powerful and quick way to focus before speaking. If you do this sense memory thoroughly enough, you'll chase the nervous thoughts out of your head.

We all get nervous, but there are ways of minimizing nerves and using the mental state to your advantage to make you a better speaker. Try them all, and pick the one or ones that works best for you.

CHAPTER SUMMARY

- The unconscious mind together with the cat-sized brain in your gut determine your emotional attitudes, which either helps you or limits you as a leader.

- You can take charge of the inner dialogues that most people have with themselves, for good or ill, by replacing negative self-talk with positive self-talk.

- Doing so will free you up for success as a leader and in life.

CHAPTER SEVEN

Synchronizing Minds

*How to Use Story to Get on
the Same Wavelength*

Here I'll discuss how you can synchronize your brain patterns with those of other people to literally get on the same wavelength with them. It's easier to do than you might think and an appropriate way to end the journey. Now you'll know how to align your nonverbal power cues with your messages, passion, and cause—and change the world.

In cool scientific prose that belies the spooky, sci-fi nature of the results, Uri Hasson, assistant professor of psychology at Princeton University, sums up his findings in a study of how people communicate: "During successful communication the speaker's and listener's brains exhibit joint, temporarily coupled, response patterns." What does that mean? It means that when people communicate successfully with one another, they get on the same wavelength. They literally match each other's brain patterns. While we're communicating, in other words, we think as one person. As Hasson says, "We're suggesting that communication is a single act performed by two brains."

He hastens to add, "It's not a Jedi mind trick. This is what communication is."[1]

Not a Jedi Mind Trick, but It Works

Perhaps Hasson is putting it the wrong way around. It would be more accurate to say that there's more to communication and less to Jedi mind tricks than we've realized up to now.

Hasson explains further: "We basically can't understand brains unless we look at the interactions between brains, since humans are social animals and so many of our behaviors involve collaboration or at least being influenced by other humans."

Here's what's going on. When a speaker begins to tell a story to a listener, their brains begin to match up. The better the story, and the better the listener understands the story, the closer the match. There's a very slight lag; that's the transmission of the sound wave (that I as the storyteller create) to the brain wave that it creates in you, the listener. When a listener understands a story particularly well, the lag goes away. In some cases, the listener's brain wave anticipates the speaker's when the listener understands the story particularly well.

So when we communicate with someone else effectively, we do something that has been described colloquially for a few generations: we get on the same wavelength. Literally. Our brain patterns match each other.

We've all had that feeling of knowing what someone else was going to say a second before he or she said it; Hasson's research shows how that can happen.

How Communication Works

The implications of Hasson's research are important and essential to understanding how communication, influence, and leadership work. I've said throughout this book that humans are social beings; we share mirror neurons that allow us to match each other's emotions directly. We anticipate and mirror each other's movements when we're in sympathy or agreement with one another—when we're on the same side. This research shows that we can mirror each other's brain activity when we're engaged in storytelling and listening.

We want to achieve this state; it's a mistake to think that most humans prefer the solitary existence that so much of modern life imposes on us. We are most comfortable when we're in communion, sharing strong emotions and stories, and led by a strong, charismatic leader who is keeping us safe and together.

If you want to lead groups of people to achieve more than any individual can achieve alone, this is how you do it. You develop a sense of how you inhabit space and modify that to fulfill the role you want to inhabit. You focus and control your emotions for key conversations, meetings, negotiations, and presentations. You harness the power of your unconscious mind to read other people reliably and quickly. You develop the leadership power of your voice, and you strengthen the non-verbal leadership signals you send out in important moments and situations. And you tap into the power of your unconscious mind to create a positive sense of what's possible for you, tuning yourself up to be ready to lead.

All of that work prepares you to put your vision across to people in powerful, persuasive ways. Then, finally, you learn how to be a storyteller who taps into the deep stories of human history and mythology to bring your message into being.

As Hasson says, again in his cool scientific tone, "I think about what I'm going to say, I produce it, and then you're listening. So I'm driving the similarities. What I'm trying to do is make your brain similar to mine. And it's not an easy process because there are many differences between us, and it's easy for you to block me. You can tune me out. So I really need you to listen to me."

Power Cue 7: Are you telling powerful stories?

The bottom line, Hasson asserts, is that "a good speaker can really take control of your brain and produce similar responses as the one he has in his brain." That's how persuasion works, in other words, inside the brain. Hasson says, "My brain is not connected to your brain, but it's producing a signal that goes into your brain."

From My Brain to Your Brain

Presto, you're a Jedi.

You've arrived at the seventh and final step in your journey to master and streamline your unconscious mind and its communication abilities. You are ready to harness the power of the unconscious mind to bring yourself to peak functioning and to lead others. This last step involves learning to learn to tell powerful stories that ensure that other people are on your wavelength.

Connecting with another human being is one of the highest forms of social being for humans. At the heart of it is good storytelling. When I'm telling you a story, and you're engaged in it, you match your brain waves to mine. If I'm telling you a story with a familiar structure, your brain actually anticipates what I'm going to say next. The point is that that's good for both parties. We *want* to be in sync with other people. It's how we communicate well with others and it's why good storytelling is so powerful. That feeling of synchronization is a profoundly satisfying one. We want to hear stories, especially ones where we can guess what's going to happen next, a split second before we're told.

Thus, when communication works, we are literally aligned with one another, down to our very brain patterns. That's both inspiring and reassuring to know; when we communicate successfully, we are actually experiencing the same thing. We are not alone.

How to Tell a Great Story

So what remains to discuss is how to tell great stories or, more precisely, how to turn your passion, your message, your vision into a great story.

Everyone seems to understand that storytelling is important, because we're awash in data and information and can't remember it all. But we do remember stories.

Stories are even more important than that. *They are how our brains work.* For example, they are why we all feel that it's safer to drive than fly, even though the statistics prove the opposite. We remember the horrifying stories of plane crashes and forget the stats. That's because we attach emotions to events to create stories and memories. Our brains are constructed that way. So storytelling is essential if you want to use the brain the way it's meant to be used. We remember the emotional, the particular, and the violent especially. We forget the boring, the general, and the anodyne.[2]

But let's start with what storytelling is *not*. Let's clear away the detritus and get to the core.

Stories Are Not about Beginnings, Middles, and Ends

My favorite wrong cliché about storytelling is the oft-cited "it has a beginning, a middle, and an end." Well, yes. But so do pencils, as my good friend from the IBM learning world, Peter Orton, is fond of saying.[3] As a definition, this one is not specific enough to be helpful. Airplane flights, dentist appointments, and pencils all have beginnings, middles, and ends, but they are not stories. They might become the fodder for stories, but stories in themselves they are not.

Forget this one. It's not helpful.

Stories Are Not Anecdotes

My next favorite spurious cliché about storytelling is that what happened the last time you visited a client site is a story. It's not, unless a conflict developed at your client site, leading to a crisis, it was resolved in some way, and someone—the hero—changed deeply and profoundly because of it. Rather, it's an anecdote. We relate anecdotes to each other all the time—*I was at the drugstore and guess who I saw? My old college buddy Aaron!* That's an anecdote, or at least the beginning of one. It may even be fascinating, but it's not a story.

Let's take a deeper example: *I met a beautiful woman at a party the other day. I shouldn't have been at the party because it was at the house of someone who doesn't like me. But the woman was beautiful.*

That's an anecdote. Here's how you turn it into a story: *I met a beautiful woman at a party the other day. I fell in love at first sight—and she with me. But when I learned her name, she turned out to be from the family of my sworn enemies. Nonetheless, we married in secret. Meeting a group of my enemies in the market the next day, I got into a fight with one of them and killed him. Now I'm banished from the city, and my wife is being pressured to marry someone else.*

That's a story, or the first part of one, and you probably recognize it: *Romeo and Juliet.*

You probably know the rest of the story, too: *Juliet takes a drug to make it look like she's dead in order to escape having to marry the other guy. Romeo doesn't get the word in time, finds her apparently dead, and kills himself. Juliet wakes up and, finding Romeo's body, kills herself.* It's a tragedy, and a story that still grabs people, five hundred years later.

Stories Are Not about You

Leaders must be authentic; that's table stakes for leadership. If you're caught being something you're not or concealing something contrary to your image, you're toast. So many, many leaders tell stories about themselves. But that's a mistake. You don't necessarily have to reveal your personal secrets to be authentic; you have to reveal your passion. The stories you tell should always make your followers, your audience, your listeners the heroes, not you. That way they allow your tribe to project itself easily into the story you're telling and they allow you to be a wise mentor or commentator. The success or failure, then, is theirs, not yours.

Stories Are Not Pretend

The final thing people most often misunderstand about storytelling has to do with story time, milk and cookies, and a rug you sat on in elementary school. Lots of people think that stories are simple, happy, trite fairy tales you tell to children. So when they hear "storytelling," they think dopey or cute. First of all, many fairy tales are terrifying and contain dark truths about the human spirit and condition, so don't underestimate them. Second, adults tell each other stories all the time, and these stories are not necessarily cute or trite, but they can be. Finally, stories loom much larger in our thinking than most people realize.

What Is a Story, Then?

What is a story? A structured way of looking at reality. A way that works for us because it matches the way our brains work.

Why should leaders tell stories? Because stories are interesting, they help people remember what you say, and they are a good way to convey information and emotion memorably. And they are so deeply ingrained in our thinking that they are the way we interpret reality.

Reality, in its raw, unfiltered, and ugly state, is chaotic. But we are not very good at dealing with chaos. Hence, we impose structures on our experiences of reality in order to make sense of it. We impose stories.

Mark Turner, a writer and philosopher who has been associated with the Institute for Advanced Study and the Center for Neural and Cognitive Sciences at the University of Maryland, says in his landmark book *The Literary Mind*, "Story is a basic principle of mind."[4]

In other words, he argues that we think in terms of stories. We learn from the high chair that if we push a glass of milk over, white liquid spills on the floor, a parent comes running making noises, mops it up, and kisses us on the top of the head (if we're lucky). That's a story, and it's a basic understanding of cause and effect by which we make sense of our world. There are actors, actions, objects, and results. It's all good fun, it's memorable, and it's how we continue to think long after we've left the high chair.

How does that apply to leaders? Most leaders communicate with their followers in lists of suggestions, demands, requests, ideas, reasons, and information. *(Five reasons to join our exciting investment company.)* Unfortunately, the human mind is not constructed to remember lists very well. Once you've told me three or four things, in order to remember the fourth or fifth I'll have to forget the first.

"In one ear and out the other" pretty much describes how we respond to lists. Yet everyone who has heard, seen, or read it once remembers the story of Romeo and Juliet. So if you act more like Shakespeare as a leader and less like the phone book, you'll be much more memorable. That's why stories are important.

How do you create a great story for the purposes of persuading and leading others? There are several steps. First, decide on the level of need. Then, figure out how your story connects to one of the five basic archetypal stories we tell one another. Finally, structure your story in a way that makes it easy for people to decide to be persuaded. Let's take those steps in order.

First, Establish a Level of Need

Abraham Maslow, an idealistic psychologist who wanted to see the positive side of people, developed a hierarchy of needs that has become an iconic pyramid. He posited five levels of need, beginning with physiological needs at the base of the pyramid, with safety next, love at the third level, esteem just above that, and self-actualization at the top.[5]

His idea was that we must satisfy those needs in order, going up the pyramid. If, in other words, we're worried about physiology or safety, we won't be thinking—or able to focus— on any levels above that, like love or esteem. His hope was that society would begin to do a better job of taking care of people and we'd gradually all work our way up the pyramid until we were all self-actualizing—working on haiku or golf or watercolors.

For leaders, the insight to take away from Maslow's hierarchy is that your potential followers' internal monologues tend to live at the safety level. Sitting in their cubes, your people are thinking things like *I wonder if my job is going to survive this downturn? I wonder if my boss hates me? I wonder if my teenage kid will survive getting his driver's license?* And so on.

So if your message is further up the pyramid, you won't grab—and hold—people's attention. You need to be somewhere near the bottom of the pyramid, talking about safety. It's why politicians running for office are always talking about security or the economy stealing your job or the like. They're trying to alarm you sufficiently at the safety level to get you to pay attention to them.

Leaders of all stripes need to do the same. But don't fake it. Make your pitch—and your level on the hierarchy—real. People are quick to spot an alarmist or a faker.

Second, Connect to an Archetype

Once you've determined the level of human need for your story, then it's time to match your idea to one of the five basic human archetypal stories. The good news is that there are only five—or maybe that's the bad news. There aren't that many to choose among. But that's the point. We experience reality, most of the time, as one of the five basic stories. We're always in one or another. So match your message to one of the five and you'll connect deeply and powerfully with your audience.[6]

For example, if you ask your employees to embark with you on a long and arduous journey to develop a new product, they'll complain about the obstacles along the way, and they may even lose heart and quit, unless you invoke a *quest* story. Then, the obstacles are to be expected because that's what happens on a quest.

Setting off on a quest. The first of the five archetypal stories, quests begin with ordinary people in an ordinary status quo situation. Then, a problem arises or an event occurs that forces the hero to leave home or depart from the status quo in order to seek some goal or right some terrible wrong and reestablish the social order. The hero's hunger for the goal is palpable. Even if the journey is long, the hero hangs in there because of the importance of reaching the goal. The heroes meet obstacles and suffer reversals, but eventually overcome them all to reach the goal.

Here's the important part. This story has lodged itself so deeply in our psyches that we don't think of it as a story. Rather, it's the way life works. If we set off on some quest, the harder we try and the worse the journey, the more we deserve the reward in the end. We believe that, because we believe in the ultimate fairness of the universe.

It's not logical. It's a story we tell ourselves. But we believe it. And that's why it's powerful.

Don't make the mistake of casting yourself as the hero. Always make your followers the hero and cast yourself as the mentor who guides the group to that goal at the end.

The quest story is the most basic one, and people will get the idea very quickly because the story is so deeply ingrained in them. For more information on the subject, read Joseph Campbell's *The Hero with a Thousand Faces*, the definitive book on the subject.[7]

After the *quest*, the other fundamental stories are: *stranger in a strange land*, *love story*, *rags to riches*, and *revenge*.

Sometimes I feel like a stranger in a strange land. A strange-land story works best in changing times. These stories are our way of handling things when everything changes—the economy, the paper mill, the rules, the demands of a global society. In a strange-land story, the heroes suddenly find themselves in a new landscape, one that offers unknown terrain, language, or rules.

We don't know the way. We're lost. What we used to do to succeed no longer makes sense any more. We're dazed and confused. We need to learn to navigate this strange new place.

Along comes a leader to show us the way. The leader (that's you) offers a new vision, a new set of rules, or a new way of coping that enables us to survive and eventually thrive in this new landscape. We crave mastery, from bewilderment, and that's the journey our leader takes us on.

Everyone needs a love story. Love stories are simple. Two people meet, fall in love, fall out of love, learn a little more about each other, decide to stick together, and live happily ever after. You know the drill. But their profundity is revealed in the nature of the way the two fall out of love and then find each other again; that's always symptomatic of what's wrong with society today. Is it the difficulties of marriage and property? That's Jane Austen. Or is it the problem of men never growing up, staying immature, and behaving badly in a society that permits them this license? That's Judd Apatow.[8]

We crave love stories because our future is tied up in them in the obvious ways, but also in not so obvious ways. If men can't learn to function like responsible adults in a world of too much grown-up play, where does that leave us? How will we take care of each other? What does society owe its people and vice versa? These are the deeper questions love stories investigate.

If you're a leader with an idea about how people need to get along better, love stories are for you.

We all go from rags to riches. Rags-to-riches stories help us believe that ordinary people still have a chance to succeed in a society that all too often seems stacked against them, in favor of the already rich and powerful. They're about average people who, with a little luck and hard work—but not genius— manage to succeed and achieve material wealth, honor, power, or fame. For people who are trying to promote economic justice, they are good stories to tell.

Finally, there's revenge. We live in a chaotic world. But we always have. Most people—throughout history—have believed that the world is the most chaotic it has ever been, right now, unlike the golden age of X years ago. There is evil in this world, and revenge reasserts the order that society all too often fails to give us from the start. We need to be protected. A good villain and justice served are powerful ways for leaders to persuade their followers that they have the right idea about life.

Again, these stories are structures that we impose on reality in order to make sense of it. If you want your message to make sense to your audiences, then you must connect it to one of these five basic stories. You might do it with a specific reference to a particular, well-known quest story, like the Holy Grail, the *Wizard of Oz*, or *Raiders of the Lost Ark*, or you might use the elements and the language of a stranger-in-a-strange-land story in order to bring your followers into that magical space without actually telling them bluntly that "you're on a quest." It's better in this case not to be blunt, but rather to evoke the stories with their unconscious power to orient us and bring us into a state of mind where we see the outcome as ordained by the structure of the story.

Put Your Specific Story Together

So you've picked one of the five basic stories. Now it's time to put your particular story together in a coherent way. My favorite structure for a persuasive message is the problem-solution structure. That's an easy one for people to get, because it begins, the way most people begin, by asking *why* and then leading your listeners to *how*. It works in this way: you begin by describing a problem that your followers have, and then you describe a solution. Then, you suggest an action for them to take to fully realize the solution. Simple, right? That's important, because simple stories are the ones that lodge in our minds, stick there, and move us to action and loyalty.[9]

Think of your story as having three acts. The first act presents an idea or a situation—a problem—that will engage your people (Romeo meets Juliet and falls in love). It's best if this idea or situation is one that, once it has happened or been told, cannot be undone. (Romeo cannot "unmeet" Juliet.) If you give your followers some information at the beginning that they don't know, it has the same effect. *(Our customer base has been eroding for the last sixteen quarters, and just today I learned that it's official—we're now down for seventeen quarters. We can't afford to go on like this . . .)* [10]

Needless to say, it should be information that is of interest to your followers; it should be about a problem they have.

The second act raises the stakes on the earlier idea or situation. (Romeo marries Juliet despite the feud between the two families.) Once again, it should be something that cannot easily be undone. *(If we have another down quarter, we're going to have to close manufacturing plants in Chicago and Ohio.)*

The third act precipitates a resolution, either favorable or unfavorable, by posing a question that must be resolved in a solution. (Romeo kills Tybalt in a duel, thus resulting in his banishment. Will Romeo and Juliet live happily ever after? Answer: no.) *(To turn things around, I'm starting a new product line, code name Lemmings, that will excite customers once again and bring them flocking back to our stores.)*

Just as no one in the play *Romeo and Juliet* ever literally asks the resolving question aloud, you don't have to in your exchanges with your followers. You do have to resolve it, and the best way is to get your people to undertake some action to enlist them in your persuasive moment. *(I've put prototype Lemmings underneath your chairs. I'd like you now to please take them out of their boxes and try them out.)*

The rest of *Romeo and Juliet* fills in around these key moments with scenes that explore the consequences of these interesting, fateful actions, and your message should too.

That's the basic structure of a good story.

But there's more. Once you've picked your story, and you're on a quest, or you've become strangers in a strange land, then you want to think about using archetypal characters to get further storytelling mileage out of our common mythology.

Don't forget Jung. Basically, an archetype is a model of a character or part of a character. The word and concept have been around for a long time, but they were made famous, so to speak, by the great Swiss psychologist Carl Jung. When Jung talked about archetypes, he meant primarily aspects of a person—the self, the shadow (your dark side), and the persona (the face you put toward the world). But he also talked about a host of other kinds of people, and aspects of people and the natural world, that could be archetypes, from the child, hero, mother, and wise old man to the fish.[11]

The idea is that your particular mother matches up with the archetypal mother in some ways and not in other ways. You may develop a mother complex as a result of a major mismatch. We live at our best and most fully when we're in harmony with all the archetypes we summon up.

Jung believed that archetypes were real—a kind of bridge between our inner psychological world and the real world out there. More than that, we all have access to universal wisdom and understanding through and with these archetypes.

So what does that mean for leaders? I think we can invoke the power of the basic archetypes by naming them at appropriate moments in our stories and by using them as ways to connect with our followers. Words like *child*, *mother*, *father*, and so on have enormous resonance for just about everyone in your tribe, whoever they are. The trick is to let your audience do the work of creating the associations by giving them enough detail to get their minds working, but not so much that you stop them from using their imaginations.

Archetypes work best in simple stories that allow audiences to fill in the blanks. You need to craft these stories—really parables—with great care so that they are not hackneyed or silly. If you do it right, you can create powerful, memorable stories—on a variety of levels—in your speeches that call people to their best, archetypal selves and move your audiences to action.

Additional Elements That All Great Stories Have

All great stories require additional elements to become truly memorable and powerful. Maybe they describe a meeting or journey, create a surprise, reveal a secret, or rely on varying levels of detail and simplicity. They might have a moral message, discuss a conflict, or describe a character's coming of age.

Great stories begin with a meeting or a journey. Great stories are all about changes—disruptions to the status quo. The classic ways in which that happens are either in meeting someone new (*Romeo and Juliet*), going on a journey (*The Odyssey*), or a combination of both (*Harry Potter and the Sorcerer's Stone*). For these approaches to work, a sense of the status quo needs to be established at the beginning of the story. Harry is stuck in a miserable existence with the Dursley family; we need to experience that for a few pages so that we can appreciate the contrast with the excitement and wonder of the new friends (and enemies) he makes and his trip to Hogwarts.

If your story doesn't begin with a meeting or a journey, then you need to look at it carefully to see if it has the necessary interest and contrast. Is there a status quo to disrupt? Has something new come along? Have things always been done in a certain way in your industry until a new product, market entrant, or idea comes along to disrupt it? Sounds like the beginning of a story to me.

Great stories have turns or surprises in them. When Romeo kills Tybalt in *Romeo and Juliet*, that's a turn or a surprise (if you're seeing it for the first time). That event is so important that it changes the direction of the story; it turns the story in another direction. Romeo has just fallen in love. He's got no reason to be killing people, especially not the family of the girl he's just fallen in love with. This is going to end badly.

Great stories let their audiences in on the secret before their characters know. This idea is a tough one for many storytellers to swallow. Instinctively, we want to surprise our audiences with startling revelations to keep their interest and to impress them with our storytelling prowess. But, there's nothing more delicious for a reader, a moviegoer, or a listener than to be in on the secret. This concept works in a couple of ways.

First, as director Alfred Hitchcock realized, there are two ways to reveal a scene to the audience. Let's say two people are talking in a café, about nothing much. You risk audience boredom unless the conversation is very, very fascinating. After a while, a bomb goes off. You give the audience a moment of shock and surprise. *Why did that happen?* Then, the scene moves on.

If, instead, you let the audience know beforehand that *a bomb is going to go off at some point in the scene*, suddenly that conversation about nothing much is exciting, suspenseful, poignant, and fascinating. When the bomb goes off, there's an awful confirmation. *The bomb* did *go off!* Much more compelling. The audience is still shocked, but it's not surprised. And it's had ten minutes of compelling moviemaking instead of ten seconds. The difference is dramatic tension. Too many story-tellers want to surprise their audiences.[12]

Second, there's a deeper kind of recognition. In the third segment of the first *Star Wars* saga, we learn that Darth Vader is Luke's father. Only the dimmest members of the audience are both surprised and shocked. We've had many hints leading up to the moment that let us in on the secret. It's still a shock when the revelation comes to Luke, but we're not surprised. We're in on the secret, and we get to watch with fascination how Luke responds.

Let your audience in on your secrets. You'll create much better stories as a result.

Stories have detail in them, but not too much. This is prob-ably the most difficult part of storytelling to get right. Most people put too much detail in their stories and drown their listeners as a result. We can't remember much detail, but just the right detail will stick in our minds forever.

Stories should be as simple as possible, but no simpler. Stories have to have enough going on in them to engage us initially and then keep our attention in a deeper way. That's why they have to connect with something archetypal and basic in human nature. Both the structure and the situation has to be at once new, that is, give us a story that hasn't been told before in precisely this way and precisely these conditions, and also familiar, that is, give us one of the archetypes.

Stories should have morals, or reinforce an important socially held belief. A good story has a moral. You don't neces-sarily have to spell it out, but you do have to make it clear. We like stories that reinforce our beliefs, in a just world, in a fair world, in a world where human endeavor leads to good results.

Conflict is at the heart of good storytelling. Without conflict, you don't have a story. But not just any conflict. It's a struggle between a hero and a villain, to put it simply. The conflict can be as big as World War III or as small as who will win the flower show. The hero can be flawed, and the villain can—and should—have his good points. But it's all about the struggle between the protagonist and antagonist.

Without that, you have an anecdote: *We were in New York City. We spotted Stanley Tucci coming out of a drugstore. We asked for his autograph. He obliged.* That's a fine celebrity-spotting anecdote, but it's not a story.

For a story to be a good one, you have to put the hero in jeopardy. That turns out to be surprisingly hard for most people—and organizations—to do, because they don't like to admit weakness, uncertainty, or anything remotely associated with flaws. Yet, it's how our hero responds to jeopardy that makes a story interesting and great.

In the recent enormously popular series of books, *The Hunger Games* (and now a major motion picture, as they say), the heart—and strength—of the trilogy is that the heroine is in terrible jeopardy for most of the three books. We get to see how Katniss struggles, fails, and deals with danger and tragedy and her own flaws, and we're mesmerized.[13]

In the business world, telling good stories is difficult because you have to get past the unwillingness of the organization to contemplate struggle, failure, and flaws. The legal department doesn't want to go there. The marketing department doesn't want to go there. But the same rules apply. No conflict, no struggle, no jeopardy—no story.

Allow your characters to change. At the heart of a great story is a hero who changes, learns, suffers, grows, *changes.* We love "coming of age" stories for that reason and, of course, love stories, not just because there's a "happily ever after" but also because the hero or heroine has learned something or grown in some way and accepted a new reality in order to win the person of his or her dreams.[14]

Stories about second chances, comebacks, sadder but wiser people—all of these compel our interest. Allowing your characters (or your company or idea or product) to change is hard because your instinct (and the advice of your legal department) is to protect your baby and keep it the same. But change wins us over. It's so much a part of human experience that to keep it out of your stories is to restrict them unnaturally and to deny them life.

Change is hard, in life and in stories, but it's essential.

How to Tell a Great Business Story: The Beginning

How can you apply these principles to the business world? In this chapter's field notes, I'll explain how to write a speech that will get a standing ovation, but for now I'll focus on the basic building blocks of any speech.

How do you begin a speech? Some recommend that you start with a joke—and even attempt it themselves. The problem with that is, for the majority of us who aren't professional comedians, it's hard to deliver jokes successfully. As any professional will tell you, most jokes fall flat. That's why they have so many comebacks up their sleeves. It's even harder to deliver a joke when you're beginning a speech, because that's when you're most nervous. So don't try it. Just don't.

Begin instead with something that will capture the audience's attention in a way that's relevant to what you're talking about. Frame the discussion in some way. You might have a startling statistic. You might have a factoid that puts things in perspective. You might have a question to ask the audience that gets its attention. You might have a personal anecdote—a well-told relevant one—that shows your interest in the subject matter. "I first became aware of the plight of Asian yak herders when I was trekking up the North Face of Everest, looked down, and saw three yaks dangling off a cliff a thousand feet below me with three herders desperately trying to get them back on the thin ribbon of trail . . ." OK, so there probably aren't yaks at that altitude on Everest, but you get the idea.

Another great way to open is to involve the people in the audience directly in some way. Challenge them to do something, ask them questions about the topic, get their input in some fashion. Try not to ask "guess what's in my head" questions or difficult questions with right and wrong answers secretly designed to show off your expertise. Instead, ask open-ended questions about the audience's experience with the topic. The point is to involve people and make them feel important and smart, not to make you feel important and smart.

Finally, you can begin with a story. Again, make it relevant to the topic. Have it frame the discussion in a way that opens up new ideas for the audience rather than closes it down. Have the story make an emotional as well as intellectual point. Tell it well. Cut out the extraneous stuff. Be clear on why the story is relevant and only include details that make the story comprehensible and refer directly to the frame.

Fundamentally, your job is to include the audience members and let them know, in the first one to three minutes, why they're there, why you're there, why the topic is important, and what your theme and emotional attitude are for that topic. If you can do that, you're off and running.

Setting Up the Right Structure

If you're going to hold people's interest in this information-saturated age, with its shrinking attention spans and increased demands on time, then you're going to have to present your case in the right way.

We've all become very smart about absorbing information, and we recognize moments when we don't have to listen. An agenda slide is one of those moments. If you start with one, you'll find that most of the people in the audience will be on their smartphones, because you haven't really started yet. They'll check out in the same way at the end, when you start your summary. Or worse, they'll ignore the middle and only listen during the summary.

Instead, begin by framing the discussion, preferably with a compelling, one-to-three-minute story or anecdote that sets up the problem but does not give the rest of the talk (or day) away. Jump right in. Horace, in his *Ars Poetica*, called it beginning in the middle of things—*in medias res*. Think about movies and TV today; they don't begin with a long list of credits. They hook you first with explosions, murders, and the like. The credits come later, if at all. That's your competition. Ignore it at your peril.

If you don't have a great story, then talk about the issue in a high-level way: "We're going to show you why widgets are not the right way to go in this market, and we're going to follow that up with some recommendations that may surprise you. We think you'll find them exciting. We're certainly excited to talk about them with you."

That's in lieu of an agenda slide.

Then, answer the question, what's in it for me?—where "me" is the audience. Go into a problem that the audience has for which your information is the solution. After you've shown the audience members that you understand their problem, then and only then are you entitled to offer your solution. If you do it in this way, you'll find happy, receptive audiences.

Connecting to a Classic Story

Let's say you're making a presentation to the board about the new product you've got in the pipeline that's going to revolutionize the marketplace and lock up profits for your company for some time. There are just one or two little glitches along the way—difficulties in production, making it hard to achieve the volume you need, and quality control issues.

These are glitches, no more. If you're on a quest, every roadblock becomes something to overcome, go around, or think your way past. The focus is on the goal, the grail, the successful product introduction. You will get there. It will be worth the effort. The team will make the necessary sacrifices to achieve the goal.

The point is to frame your briefing in these terms, with these overtones playing throughout the talk. It will be more effective if you don't say, "We're on a quest," but rather talk in terms of the conditions, features, and goals of a quest. Your anecdotes can be miniature quests or pieces of them, and your call to action at the end can be a stirring paean to enlist the team in the fun, with grand allusions to your favorite historical quests, whether Biblical, Greek, or a drive for some half-remembered pennant.

Let's say you're explaining to the troops how the changing marketplace has rendered half of your services irrelevant. A combination of new regulation, new market entrants, and global paranoia is making it very difficult to figure out how to continue along the successful path of rising profits that has sustained your company so well in the past decade.

What you want to say is that although the world has changed, it will be the disciplined application of the basic formula for business success that launched the company to begin with that will help the team now. So while conditions are different and it appears that a whole new set of rules should apply, it's really a matter of recognizing what hasn't changed in the mix in order to point the way toward success.

That's the classic stranger-in-a-strange-land story. You're suddenly surrounded by unfamiliar terrain and the going is rough. So you take a deep breath and start to explore. As you get to know the new place you find yourself in, you gradually recognize that certain old skills will stand you in very good stead. Other, newer habits you had picked up during your years of success need to be tossed away. It's time to get back to business basics.

Once again, you want to focus on the confusion first; that's the basic condition for a strange-land story. Make it as disorienting as you can. Get lost in the new strange trees with your audience. Get them worked up with the confusion you've felt and even the despair you've experienced as you watched the profit margins begin to erode and weren't sure what exactly to do about them.

Then, you move to the recognition and the compelling reminder to your audience of the timeless truths with which the business began, as you point out the new clarity you've achieved about the road ahead. There is no Holy Grail or no end point here as in a quest; what's needed a constant return to the basics, an ongoing effort to stay disciplined, focused, and aware of the changing new conditions.

Good storytelling isn't easy. It's not easy to step aside and make someone else the hero of a story you're passionate about. It's not easy to dwell in the problem that the hero is dealing with. It's not easy to be honest about the challenges your hero is going to face along the way to fixing that problem. But if you do it right, you will connect with your audience in a powerful, almost electrical way. You will beam your passion from your brain into theirs. You will pull off a Jedi mind trick.

FIELD NOTES

Getting to the Standing Ovation

You know you want one—a standing ovation. Speakers don't like to admit that they're so needy, but let's be honest. You put yourself and your ideas on the line; who wouldn't want to close on a roar of approval and an audience that surges to its feet to express its love and admiration?

So here's how to get one, in five easy steps.

1. **Begin with a compelling framing story.** This is not an anecdote about your trip to the venue or a story about your kids. It's a compelling, brief narrative making the general problem you're talking about concrete and interesting. If you're talking to an internal audience about declining customer satisfaction, say, then you want a story about a specific customer who was

---

unhappy because of something an employee did or didn't do. Make the narrative more than one minute and less than three minutes long.

2. **Then talk about a problem the audience has.** The guts of any "standing O" talk are not information; they are sharing your perspective on a problem the audience has. It's all about the audience. That's so crucial, I'll say it again: it's about the audience, not about you. You want to delve deep into the problem, on both intellectual and emotional levels. To get that standing O, you're going to have to focus on the emotional response of the audience to the problem.

3. **Involve the audience in analyzing the problem.** This is a crucial step. You want to get the audience members participating in the discussion of the problem. Ask for their input, their stories, their understanding. Break them up into small groups if necessary, but figure out some way to get them doing some of the work.

4. **Then show the people in the audience how they can solve the problem.** This is where you get to be most didactic—and helpful. Share your expertise with the audience to solve the problem. But just as crucially, figure out a way for people to get involved here, too. Set the broad outline of the solution, and then let them fill in some details.

5. **Close with a call to action that involves the audience.** The trick here is to finish strong, using the magic word "you" where "you" is the audience. "Together, we can do this, and you will be the first team to achieve XXXX in the history of YYYY. Is that not worth a few long nights? Let's get started!"

And they're on their feet. A standing O comes about because people want to give energy back, because they're inspired by the speaker. Applauding is the first way to do that, but standing is a more energetic way and therefore more satisfying—for them. *All you have to do is make it about them, let them get involved—and get your own ego out of the way.*

CHAPTER SUMMARY

- When we tell each other stories, our brain patterns synchronize.

- That synchronization enables good communication.

- You can increase the likelihood that people will listen to you as a leader by telling stories.

- To tell a great story, first understand what it is not.

- Then make sure your story is pitched at a level of need that will grab your audience.

- Tell one of five basic stories from deep within our archetypal thinking: quest, stranger in a strange land, love story, rags to riches, or revenge.

- Tell a great story in three acts.

- Telling a great story is more art than science; you must invoke emotions.

Community and Communication

Radical Authenticity

Modern brain research puts us in touch with a far more powerful understanding of the way that humans communicate than we've had before. We are hard-wired to join up and communicate together through our unconscious minds. Our evolutionary past necessitated this confluence of communication, and we need to get in touch with it again in order to realize the full power of influence an individual can have over a group. At the same time, the radical connectivity of the digital revolution has necessitated significant changes in the way we communicate with one another.

In Ancient Fiesole, There Is an Amphitheater

In the hills above Florence, Italy, is an ancient town founded by the Romans or maybe the Etruscans before them. Fiesole is perched on a tiny summit with views that stretch forever in all

231

directions. In the middle of the town are the ruins of Roman baths and an amphitheater.

A few years ago, I stood on the stage of that theater, orating to an invisible crowd, hearing the amazing acoustics as my voice echoed around me, and thinking about the rhetorical and communications wisdom that the Romans and Greeks have passed down to us.

They understood that the audience is the most important part of any communication. Amphitheaters go up to the audience, not down. The stage is the lowest point.

They understood that there was something sacred about gathering, ritual, and storytelling. Amphitheaters are open to the sky. Human ritual begins in communal acts of coming together to understand essential events, the passage of time and season, life and death.

They understood that any presentation has to begin by answering a key question for that specific audience: Why does this matter? Why is what the speaker is going to say important? When you collect people in an amphitheater, the grandeur of the setting demands an immediate answer to that question of why.

They understood that only once you've oriented the audience in this way, can you tell them the *what* and the *how*—in that order. Once you've set such a stage, then you must deliver something of import.

They understood the importance of community to communications. We gather together to communicate because only in that way can we share in the emotions and the journey as one.

So they understood sight and sound. Every single seat in the amphitheater in Fiesole has a perfect view of the stage. And the brilliant acoustics mean that you can be heard from any point on the stage anywhere in the audience.

The Ancients Understood the
Importance of Presence

These ancient orators were masters of the communications challenges of their day. Now we have to learn anew how to be masters of our communications issues in this complicated twenty-first century. We can draw on some ancient wisdom; after all, some things haven't changed. But we also need modern brain research and experience to help us the rest of the way to mastery, because the sturdy common sense of the ancient Greeks and Romans doesn't always hold up to scrutiny in the modern era. Not all of their advice is useful in our helter-skelter, information-overloaded world.

The combination of ancient, amphitheater-tested wisdom and hard science brings us to a place we've never been able to reach before: complete mastery of personal communications. Because communication is the beginning of leadership, the techniques in this book will propel you to new levels of leadership.

How do you show up when you walk into a room? Take control of your presence and change both your thinking and the messages you send to those around you.

What emotions do you convey for important meetings, conversations, and presentations? Share your focused emotions and control the emotional tenor of your tribe.

What unconscious messages are you receiving from others? Use your unconscious expertise to stay attuned to the hidden messages of everyone around you.

Do you have a leadership voice? Tune your voice to automatically lead your peers.

What honest signals do you send out in key work and social situations? Establish the right levels of energy and passion to win the contract, the negotiation, or the raise.

Is your unconscious mind holding you back or propelling you forward? Shed your unconscious mind of the blocks and impediments to success.

Are you telling powerful stories? Convey your message in ways that ensure that your listeners are aligned with you, down to their very brain waves.

Communication Has Changed in Three Ways

Twenty-first century communication has changed how we connect to the world in three essential ways: connectivity, authenticity, and style. The first way is obvious to any sentient being within reach of the digital world. As Nicco Mele notes in his brilliant book about the darker implications of the digital revolution, *The End of Big*, "Radical connectivity—our breathtaking ability to send vast amounts of data instantly, constantly, and globally—has all but transformed politics, business, and culture, bringing about the upheaval of traditional, 'big' institutions and the empowerment of upstarts and renegades."[1]

I like Mele's phrase, "radical connectivity," because it gets at what's truly different in ways that words and phrases like the *internet* and *social media* do not. They are the media; radical connectivity is the result. By putting us all within one or two removes from one another, the digital era has radically flattened hierarchies of communication everywhere and completely reshaped the old power relationship between the rulers and the masses. Now, a single furious customer can close a restaurant, a single, impassioned person can ignite support for a cause, and a single disgruntled citizen can start a movement and bring down a government.

This shift has two implications for communications. First, it necessarily increases the volume and dumbs down the sophistication of the information flow. That's the bad news: there's more to wade through now and a lot of it isn't pretty. Second, anyone's voice can get heard and perhaps even get the hearing it deserves. That's the good news. You're competing with dancing nerds, phony news, and cute cats, but if you persist, your story will most likely be heard.

In a Radically Connected World, Be Persistent and Smart

Another way that communications has changed in the twenty-first century is that we now demand authenticity in a way we haven't before. Let's call it "radical authenticity" to go with the radical connectivity.

Let's be clear: this new radical authenticity is hard. It's hard because it *is* hard to be open and honest about ourselves, warts and all. It's hard because sometimes we want to hide our less than perfect traits from ourselves. And it's hard because other people may seize on our weaknesses as proof of our unworthiness, rather than our humanity.

Suddenly, it's all out there. Are you ready for that?

Authenticity is the most important quality in leadership communications. With it, you can move people to action. Without it, you can't even get a hearing. We think what makes us human is our uniqueness, but it's really our commonalities. We can lose track of our essence in daily compromises, accommodations, and dealings. Most of us are growing into ourselves; we're not already complete beings.

Suddenly, it's all out there, and no one can be fully ready for that.

Radical authenticity means managing your body language. As I've said, every communication is two conversations. The first conversation in every face-to-face communication is the one you're aware of: the spoken content. The second conversation is the one on which most humans are unconscious experts: the nonverbal one.

It's the nonverbal conversation that will make or break you as a communicator. That's really what's radical about the new authenticity. Faking it won't work anymore, at least not for the long haul. The nonverbal conversation is where authenticity is created or destroyed. It may confirm you as the top dog, sabotage your authority, blow your chances at getting a raise or get you the big sale, lose you the prize or win it—and on and on through most of the big moments in life.

Understanding and *controlling* this second conversation are key to leadership, because they are not something that you can leave to chance or the unconscious. There are simply too many decisions to be made, too many inputs to weigh, too many people to manage and lead. In the twenty-first century, the pace of leadership has accelerated, the flow of information has exploded, and the physical and intellectual demands on leaders have intensified.

So you can no longer rely on common sense or instinct or winging it as you once might have done. With camcorders and YouTube everywhere, you have to assume that your life as a leader is almost entirely transparent. Leaders who rely on ad-libbing and improvisation risk looking unprepared and stilted. The irony of leadership in the media age is that winging it looks fake; only the prepared can look authentic. This paradox raises the stakes on our cave-person communication skills. We can no longer leave the second conversation—the source of radical authenticity—to the unconscious, to chance, and to the moment.

Radical authenticity means preparing for the moment, not just being in it. What we all do, as unconscious experts of the nonverbal communication of emotions, is ascribe intent to what we see. We don't think to ourselves, *Oh, I see a slumped shoulder and a bowed head. I sense trouble.* Instead, we jump immediately to intent, decoding what we see: *Uh-oh, Jones is in trouble. This could be bad.*

That's precisely because this expertise developed over eons in order to keep us alive and functioning in the tribe. We had to learn to respond instantly to nonverbal cues because by the time they became conscious, it was too late.

That instant, unconscious response is less useful in the modern era, when we have to do civilized things like lead thousands of people to action, manage groups of employees, and have conversations with discouraged coworkers. Here, our natural tendencies to self-preservation can get in the way. Defensiveness, which makes perfect sense when you are about to have a confrontation with a saber-toothed tiger, creates a bad feeling when you are trying to lead a team of software engineers. Fight-or-flight reactions of hostility, rapid heart rates, and flared nostrils don't serve us well when the boss says, "How are you going to accomplish *X* in time frame *Y*?" They would have been fine when fleeing a woolly mammoth, but it's no longer the case.

Authenticity is hard because we think it's all about being, but it's really all about doing. We have to learn to do new things that our unconscious minds or evolution haven't prepared us for.

Radical authenticity means using your instincts consciously. Because our instincts can betray us, we have to learn how to manage them. We must be able to have the two conversations together in a controlled, useful, conscious way. That's the essence of leadership communications, and it's a tall order. How can we make the unconscious conscious without losing spontaneity, power, and the appearance of ease?

Here's where the paradox of leadership comes in. Because we humans tend to interpret fumbling, hesitations, and sloppiness as evidence of lack of preparedness, inauthenticity, and amateurishness, the leaders who wing it instead of preparing always fail to impress. The ones who rehearse, role-play, and prepare with real passion are the ones who connect with their public, their audiences, and their followers—and appear authentic.

- Authenticity is essential because it's the only way to do good work.

- Authenticity is essential because our children need to learn it from us.

- Authenticity is essential because without it, there is no core.

- Authenticity is essential because if we open up about our weaknesses other people won't bother.

- Authenticity is essential because it's how we grow into ourselves.

- Authenticity is essential because otherwise we'll compromise once too often and lose our way for good.

- Authenticity is essential because life is too short for anything else.

Radical authenticity means making what's staged look impromptu. We want authentic people as leaders, and what the world doesn't realize is how hard it is to appear that way. It takes an understanding of how communications works and practice. There's nothing spontaneous about authenticity in this televised age.

So how do you show up with predetermined authenticity? What about that irony of practicing authenticity? Doesn't that mean that any such "authenticity" will be fake?

Thinking about it in this way mistakes what it is and how it is projected. Authenticity is genuineness. The shortcut we use to determine it in the people around us is *consistency* in message and body language—does this person appear to mean what she says?

So the irony is that the more you practice being consistent, the more likely you are to show up that way. When people don't rehearse, they send out unconscious messages with their bodies that *this is the first time I'm doing this.* The body language cues of first-timers overlap with the cues of people who don't fully mean what they say. Both groups tend to engage in self-protective behavior because they feel exposed. Both groups telegraph nervousness through agitated body language. Both groups often restrict their own motion and movement to make themselves feel safer. The result signals to the people around us (unconsciously) that the leader is not relaxed, fluid, and at ease.

So the way to look authentic—radically authentic—is to practice. Your body must get the muscle memory of standing, walking, and talking in the ways that it will during the real event or occasion. If it does, then it can show up with some authority and presence, and your tribe will interpret that as authenticity, if the (more comfortable) body language does in fact match the message. That is the kind of important issue that gets answered by rehearsal.

If you rehearse, you and your body can focus on the moment when you're actually delivering your message. That greatly increases the chances that you'll show up as authentic.

In a Radically Connected World, Personal Authenticity Is Table Stakes

Another way that communications has changed in the twenty-first century is style. The development of leadership communications has paralleled the development of acting.

Stage acting in the Victorian period would now seem bizarrely and hilariously stylized to us. The technique was based on a gestural vocabulary that included drawing back, with both hands open and raised up, eyes wide open, and mouth agape to indicate surprise and that sort of thing. Actors would adopt stances that were familiar to their audiences to show the various emotions they wished to convey.

Some of the gestures have survived in the language of mime, but otherwise they've been forgotten, except perhaps as jokey, exaggerated reactions in slapstick routines or in charades.

What's happened is that succeeding generations of actors strove to make acting more and more natural, that is, more closely mimicking real human behavior. The evolution of first stage and then movie acting has proceeded to such a point that even a great actor of a couple of generations ago, like Sir Laurence Olivier, now appears to us stiff and overly mannered. Try watching his version of *Hamlet* and you'll see what I mean.

Leadership communications has undergone the same evolution at the top echelons, but the word hasn't trickled down to everyone yet. The result is that communication habits that were acceptable in the last quarter of the twentieth century now seem overly formal and stagey to us.

What people crave is a conversation—and a conversational style—from their leaders.

Television is partly to blame, but mostly it's the parallel evolution of leadership communications to a more natural style. Because television has brought our leaders, politicians, and speakers up close, as if they were in our living rooms, we now demand that they talk to us like our neighbors might. Anything else seems fake, pompous, or over the top.

Leaders today need to focus on having a conversation with their followers. Keep it natural, as natural as you can be. Natural is still a style, but it's an evolving one, and leaders have to keep up with the times just like actors.

With one caveat: when leaders deliberately adopt high rhetorical phrasing, the effect is to create a sense of high seriousness. If the leader carries it off, without becoming pompous or boring, then the result can be very powerful. In truth, both kinds of speech are available to the leader, if used with care.

Similarly, conversational phrasing can become too trite for the occasion, just as more elegant flights of rhetoric can go over the top. We still have a sense that, during important civic moments, leaders should show their sense of the occasion by upping the rhetorical ante.

What is the appropriate language of public discourse? It's anybody's to influence, to create, to master. The key test is always authenticity. That's what we demand of our leaders first, last, and always.

In a Radically Connected World, Your Style Has to Include Listening

It's time to stop letting our unconscious minds decide our careers, our relationships, our lives. It's time for us to take charge consciously of the human cues and connections that have evolved over millions of years, so that we can become fully conscious beings, in control of ourselves and our destinies.

Do you want to become a leader in your life, or do you want it simply to happen to you?

What's needed from leaders is simple: people want to belong and to be led, just as they always have. What's complicated today is leadership execution—to control your unconscious mind successfully involves lots of moving parts.

But now you're able, for the first time, to integrate the power of your unconscious mind into your conscious life—your leadership life. The power is there, waiting for you to take it. You know the power cues. You know how to harness your unconscious and make it serve your conscious life rather than betray or undercut it.

It's not an easy assignment. Of course, it never has been. But it is particularly difficult now. The leadership stakes have been raised, again and again. But the game has never been more worth playing.

Communication is global, instant, and digital. But that doesn't change the need people have for tribes. What happens is that we learn to pick and choose the information we want from the vast stream that goes past us every second of every day. We identify with selected aspects of the torrent of modern life in order to define who we are—and who we are not.

That simply makes the need for tribal identification more important.

At the same time, attention spans keep shrinking. *Say it fast or don't bother. But keep it real. And tell me something I don't know.* So, the ante for public communication keeps getting raised, and leadership keeps getting harder and harder because of that.

In spite of this torrent of communication, or perhaps because of it, there's a desperate shortage of leaders who are willing to listen, deeply and with integrity, to their tribes. Apparently, the Chinese character for listening is made up of other characters (or perhaps traces of characters) for the ear, the eye, and the heart. That surely suggests something vital about listening: it needs to involve all three. Listening is a skill that is in appallingly short supply in this era of overstimulation and information overload.[2]

We need to listen to each other more, and more deeply. We need to hear, appreciate, and learn about each other's stories. If you don't think so, ask yourself this: When are you, as a leader, going to start paying attention? How are you going to make the time to listen? And how are you going to create the capacity to listen?

In the end, leadership is listening.

We need to listen to each other because life is precious and short. We need to listen to each other because despite our superficial disagreements and differences, we are still the best hope and the gravest danger for the planet we call home. We need to listen to each other because we need to work together in peace in order to build a better world.

Most of all, we need to listen to each other because lives need to be shared, we are a communal species, and isolation kills.

When you listen as a leader, you should listen with your whole body. Use your ears, of course, but also use your eyes and your heart. Listen for the facts, of course, but also listen for the underlying emotions and values of the other person. Only when you listen *that* carefully and deeply can you begin to understand and then communicate with someone else. I don't know if the Chinese character for listening really does include the characters for the ear, the eye, and the heart, but I do know that *listening* needs to include all those things. Let's start listening better to one another and maybe—just maybe—we can save this magical planet and the precious, irreplaceable people on it.

NOTES

INTRODUCTION

1. Noel Barber, *The Flight of the Dalai Lama* (London: Hodder & Stoughton, 1960).

2. E. M. Forster, *Maurice: A Novel* (London: Edward Arnold, 1971).

3. A. K. Pradeep, *The Buying Brain: Secrets for Selling to the Subconscious Mind* (Hoboken, NJ: Wiley, 2010), 4.

4. Vijay Balasubramanian, Kristin Koch, Peter Sterling, Judith MacLean, Michael A. Freed, Ronen Segev, and Michael J. Berry III, "How Much the Eye Tells the Brain," *Current Biology*, July 2006.

5. Antonio R. Damasio, *Self Comes to Mind: Constructing the Conscious Brain* (New York: Pantheon Books, 2010).

6. Eric R. Kandel, *In Search of Memory: The Emergence of a New Science of Mind* (New York: W.W. Norton & Co., 2006).

7. Anne Karpf, *The Human Voice: How This Extraordinary Instrument Reveals Essential Clues about Who We Are* (New York: Bloomsbury Publications/Holtzbrinck, 2006).

8. Alex Pentland with Tracy Heibeck, *Honest Signals: How They Shape Our World* (Cambridge, MA: MIT Press, 2008).

9. Jose Drost-Lopez, "The Neural Spark," September 20, 2010, http://decodethemind.wordpress.com/2010/09/10/more-brain-connections-than-stars-in-the-universe-no-not-even-close/.

10. Thomas Lewis, Fari Amini, and Richard Lannon, *A General Theory of Love* (New York: Random House, 2000); see also Susan Goldin-Meadow, *Hearing Gesture: How Our Hands Help Us Think* (Cambridge, MA: Belknap Press of Harvard University Press, 2003), for a deeper treatment of how gesture interacts with thought, especially in teaching children; Giacomo Rizzolatti and Corrado Sinigaglia, *Mirrors in the Brain: How Our Minds Share Actions and Emotions,* trans. Frances Anderson (Oxford and New York: Oxford University Press, 2008); V. S. Ramachandran, *A Brief Tour of Human Consciousness: From Imposter Poodles to Purple Numbers* (New York: Pi Press, 2004); Karpf, *The Human Voice*; Stanford Gregory Jr., with Timothy Gallagher, "Spectral Analysis of Candidates' Non-verbal Vocal Communication," *Social Psychology Quarterly*, 2002; Michael D. Gershon, *The Second Brain: The Scientific Basis of Gut Instinct and a Groundbreaking New Understanding of Nervous Disorders of the Stomach and Intestine* (New York: HarperCollins, 1998); Pentland, *Honest Signals*; Uri Hasson, "Princeton University: Case Study on Brains and 'Dyadic Social Interactions,'" http://psych.princeton.edu/psychology/research/hasson/case.php#casestudy2.

11. Niccolò Machiavelli, *The Prince and Selected Discourses*, trans. Daniel Donno (New York: Bantam Books, 1966).

12. See, for example, Leil Lowndes, *Undercover Sex Signals: A Pickup Guide for Guys* (New York: Citadel, 2006).

13. Michael C. Corballis, *From Hand to Mouth: The Origins of Language* (Princeton, NJ: Princeton University Press, 2002).

14. Valorie N. Salimpoor, Mitchel Benovoy, Kevin Larcher, Alain Dagher, and Robert J. Zatorre, "Anatomically Distinct Dopamine Release During Anticipation and Experience of Peak Emotion to Music," *Nature Neuroscience* 14, January 2011.

CHAPTER 1

1. Hal Pashler, Mark McDaniel, Doug Rohrer, and Robert Bjork, "Learning Styles Debunked," *Psychological Science in the Public Interest*, December 2009.

2. Loukia D. Loukopoulos, R. Key Dismukes, and Immanuel Barshi, *The Multitasking Myth: Handling Complexity in Real-World Operations* (Burlington, VT: Ashgate Pub. Ltd., 2009).

3. Hans Hass, *The Human Animal: The Mystery of Man's Behavior*, trans. J. Maxwell Brownjohn (New York: Putnam, 1970).

4. Nick Morgan, *Trust Me: Four Steps to Authenticity and Charisma* (San Francisco, CA: Jossey-Bass, 2009).

5. Desmond Morris, *The Naked Ape: A Zoologist's Study of the Human Animal* (London: Cape, 1967).

6. Joseph Murphy, *The Power of Your Subconscious Mind* (New York: Jeremy P. Tarcher/Penguin, 2010).

7. Susan Goldin-Meadow, phone interview by author, April 20, 2012. All quotes in this chapter from the interview.

8. Thomas Lewis, Fari Amini, and Richard Lannon, *A General Theory of Love* (New York: Random House, 2000).

9. Ibid.

10. Goldin-Meadow, phone interview by author, April 20, 2012.

11. V. S. Ramachandran, *A Brief Tour of Human Consciousness: From Imposter Poodles to Purple Numbers* (New York: Pi Press, 2004).

12. Goldin-Meadow, phone interview by author, April 20, 2012.

13. Ibid.

14. Vintage 1970s TV commercial, "When E. F. Hutton Talks, People Listen," http://www.youtube.com/watch?v=2MXqb1a3Apg.

CHAPTER 2

1. Susan Goldin-Meadow, phone interview by author, April 20, 2012.

2. Constantin Stanislavski, *An Actor Prepares*, trans. Elizabeth Reynolds Hapgood (New York: Theatre Arts, 1936).

3. Amy Cuddy, "Your Body Language Shapes Who You Are," TED talk video, filmed June 2012, posted October 2012, http://www.ted.com/talks/amy_cuddy_your_body_language_shapes_who_you_are.html.

NOTES

4. Giacomo Rizzolatti and Corrado Sinigaglia, *Mirrors in the Brain: How Our Minds Share Actions and Emotions*, trans. Frances Anderson (Oxford and New York: Oxford University Press, 2008).
5. Ibid., 190–191.
6. Ibid., 192–193.
7. Thomas Lewis, Fari Amini, and Richard Lannon, *A General Theory of Love* (New York: Random House, 2000).
8. V. S. Ramachandran, *A Brief Tour of Human Consciousness: From Imposter Poodles to Purple Numbers* (New York: Pi Press, 2004).
9. President Clinton apparently said this to an AIDS activist in 1992. See http://en.wikiquote.org/wiki/Bill_Clinton.
10. A. K. Pradeep, *The Buying Brain: Secrets for Selling to the Subconscious Mind* (Hoboken, NJ: Wiley, 2010).

CHAPTER 3

1. Paul Ekman, ed., *Emotional Awareness: Overcoming the Obstacles to Psychological Balance and Compassion: A Conversation between the Dalai Lama and Paul Ekman* (New York: Times Books, 2008).
2. Ibid.
3. Paul Ekman, *Telling Lies: Clues to Deceit in the Marketplace, Politics, and Marriage* (New York: W.W. Norton, 1985).
4. Desmond Morris, *Peoplewatching: The Desmond Morris Guide to Body Language* (New York: Vintage, 2002).
5. A. K. Pradeep, *The Buying Brain: Secrets for Selling to the Subconscious Mind* (Hoboken, NJ: Wiley, 2010).
6. Mark L. Knapp, Judith A. Hall, and Terrence G. Horgan, *Nonverbal Communication in Human Interaction*, 8th ed. (Boston: Wadsworth, Cengage Learning, 2014).
7. Ibid.
8. Ibid.
9. Ekman, *Telling Lies*.
10. Shunryū Suzuki, ed. Trudy Dixon, *Zen Mind, Beginner's Mind* (Boston: Shambhala, 2006).

CHAPTER 4

1. Frank Herbert, *Dune* (New York: Ace Books, 2005).
2. Colin H. Hansen, ed., *The Effects of Low-Frequency Noise and Vibration on People* (Brentwood, UK: Multi-Science Publishing Co., 2007).
3. J. W. S. Rayleigh, *The Theory of Sound*, vols. 1 and 2, 2nd ed. (London: Macmillan and Co., Ltd., 1937); for the basics; see also Don Campbell and Alex Doman, *Healing at the Speed of Sound: How What We Hear Transforms Our Brains and Our Lives* (New York: Hudson Street Press, 2011).
4. Stanford Gregory, phone interview by author, April 16, 2012. All quotes by Gregory are from this interview.

5. Ibid.

6. Ibid.

7. Cara C. Tigue, Diana J. Borak, Jillian J. M. O'Connor, Charles Schandl, and David R. Feinberg, "Voice Pitch Influences Voting Behavior," *Evolution and Human Behavior* 33, no. 3 (May 2012).

8. Donna Farhi, *The Breathing Book: Good Health and Vitality through Essential Breath Work* (New York: Henry Holt, 1996).

9. Gregory, phone interview by author, April 16, 2012.

10. Jody Kreiman and Diana Sidtis, *Foundations of Voice Studies: An Interdisciplinary Approach to Voice Production and Perception* (Malden, MA: Wiley-Blackwell, 2011).

11. Listen to President Reagan's speech on the *Challenger* disaster, January 28, 1986, http://www.youtube.com/watch?v=Qa7icmqgsow.

12. Patsy Rodenburg, *Presence: How to Use Positive Energy for Success in Every Situation* (London: Michael Joseph, 2007), and Patsy Rodenburg, *The Right to Speak: Working with the Voice* (New York: Routledge, 1992).

13. See, for example, the chapters on the war years in Martin Gilbert, *Churchill: A Life* (London: Heinemann, 1991).

14. Ewen Callaway, "Male Voices Reveal Owner's Strength," *New Scientist* 2765 (June 2010).

CHAPTER 5

1. Alex Pentland with Tracy Heibeck, *Honest Signals: How They Shape Our World* (Cambridge, MA: MIT Press, 2008), 1–19.

CHAPTER 6

1. Heribert Watzke, "The Brain in Your Gut," TED talk video, filmed July 2010, posted October 2010, http://www.ted.com/talks/heribert_watzke_the_brain_in_your_gut.html.

2. Michael D. Gershon, *The Second Brain: The Scientific Basis of Gut Instinct and a Groundbreaking New Understanding of Nervous Disorders of the Stomach and Intestine* (New York: HarperCollins, 1998); and phone interview by author, April 6, 2012.

3. R. Joseph, *Limbic System: Amygdala, Hippocampus, Hypothalamus, Septal Nuclei, Cingulate, Emotion, Memory, Sexuality, Language, Dreams, Hallucinations, Unconscious Mind* (Lanham, MD: University Press, Rowman & Littlefield, 2011).

4. Tony Morris, Michael Spittle, and Anthony P. Watt, *Imagery in Sport* (Champaign, IL: Human Kinetics, 2005).

5. Rhonda Byrne, *The Secret* (New York: Atria Books, 2006).

CHAPTER 7

1. Uri Hasson, interview by author, May 11, 2012. All quotes in this chapter are from this interview.

2. Mark Turner, *The Literary Mind* (New York: Oxford University Press, 1996).

NOTES

3. Peter Orton, phone interview by author, January 2012.

4. Turner, *The Literary Mind*.

5. Joseph Campbell, *The Hero with a Thousand Faces*, 3rd ed. (Novato, CA: New World Library, 2008).

6. Ibid.

7. Ibid.

8. Judd Apatow, *The 40 Year Old Virgin*, Universal Pictures, 2005.

9. Halford Ryan, *Classical Communication for the Contemporary Communicator* (Mountain View, CA: Mayfield Pub. Co., 1992).

10. Bernard D. N. Grebanier, *Playwriting* (New York: Crowell, 1961).

11. C. G. Jung, *The Archetypes and the Collective Unconscious*, trans. R. F. C. Hull (New York: Pantheon, 1959).

12. Sidney Gottlieb, ed., *Hitchcock on Hitchcock: Selected Writings and Interviews* (Berkeley: University of California Press, 1995).

13. Suzanne Collins, *The Hunger Games* (New York: Scholastic Press, 2008).

14. Grebanier, *Playwriting*.

CONCLUSION

1. Nicco Mele, *The End of Big: How the Internet Makes David the New Goliath* (New York: St. Martin's Press, 2013).

2. For an explanation of the Chinese character for listening, see the US Department of State website: http://www.state.gov/m/a/os/65759.htm#.UHY fyS6uizI.

INDEX

activity, 146, 147, 148–149, 157–158
actors, 240–241
  method acting, 56–59
  vocal control of, 133
adrenaline, 75, 77, 141, 180–181,
  197–198
alignment, 92–93
  body language indicating, 98–99
  of brain waves, 16, 17
  creating, 115–117
  with leaders, 124–126
  mirroring and, 155
anecdotes, 206–207
archetypes, 210–214, 216–217, 224–226
Ars Poetica (Horace), 223
attention, limits to, 53–55
attention spans, 24–25, 162, 223, 243
authenticity, 231–244
  charisma and, 61
  emotion and, 112
  instinct and, 238–239
  manipulation versus, 22
  method acting and, 61
  preparedness and, 236–238
  presence and, 65–67
  radical, 235–240
  storytelling and, 14, 207
authoritative arc, 134–135
authority
  challenging, 152
  dominance and, 150–151
  passion and, 152–153
  positional, 152
  verbal tics and, 135–137

Bell Labs, 122
body language
  alignment indicated by, 98–99,
  115–117

authenticity and, 236–237
baseline readings of, 93–94, 104
confidence and, 45–46
constellations of, 92–93, 113
diary of, 43–45
friend versus foe, 92–93, 97–98
intent and, 90
learning to read others', 88–118
leg and foot movements, 95
of listening, 101–103
method acting and, 56–59
of power, 92–93, 95–97
practical implications of, 5–6
practicing changes in, 240
in public speaking, 167–173
self-awareness of, 9
space zones and, 79–80
spoken content versus, 27
thought led by, 75
Boehner, John, 159, 161
"Brain in Your Gut, The" (Watzke), 178
brain waves. *See also* neuroscience
  alignment of with others, 16, 17
  desire for alignment of, 17
  gesture/word mismatches and, 37
  synchronization of, 13–14, 201–229
breathing, 76–77
  diaphragmatic, 129–130
  public speaking and, 198
  voice and, 128–130, 141

Campbell, Joseph, 212
charisma
  authenticity and, 66–67
  developing, 60–61
  focusing emotions in, 48, 59–61
  mastery and, 48
  method acting for projecting,
  56–59

charisma (*continued*)
  passion and, 67
  presence and, 41, 43–45
  projecting, 9
  projecting to crowds, 70–72
  self-assessment of, 47–48
  storytelling and, 13–14
  voice and, 137–138
chi, 179–181
Churchill, Winston, 139
Clinton, Bill, 65
Clinton, Hillary, 159, 160–161
cognitive load, 37–38, 54–55
commitment, 163
communalism, 18–21, 231–233,
  242–243
communication
  authenticity in, 231–244
  changes in modern, 234–244
  empathy in, 64–65
  focusing on nonverbal, 5–6
  honest signals in, 145–174
  importance of gestures in, 28–30,
    33–34
  misconceptions about, 23–25
  research on, 15–17
  role of emotion in, 111
  simultaneous conversations in, 27–30
  as storytelling, 204–205
  taking control of, 8–9
  unconscious, 6–8
  virtual, honest signals in, 161–166
confidence, 16
  honest signals and, 150
  mastery and, 48
  method acting to project, 57–59
  self-assessment of, 45–46
  voice and, 128
conservation test, 35–36
consistency, 147, 149–150, 158–159,
  239–240
context, 94
conversations. *See also* communication
  with audiences, 142–143
  importance of gestures in, 28–30
  influence and, 153–154
  leadership, 138–140, 241–242

listening in, 101–103
power indicators in, 95–96
simultaneous verbal and nonverbal,
  27–30
telephone, 123–124
conviction, 151

Daily Show, The (TV show), 96
Dalai Lama, 1–3, 83–85
decision making, 13
  ability to process emotions and, 16
  doubts in, concealing, 139
  emotions in, 63–64
  unconscious, 7
defensiveness, 71–72, 101
deLontrey, Pierre, 122–123
demands, 209
distractedness, projecting, 55–56
dominance, 150–151. *See also* leaders
  and leadership
Dune (Herbert), 120

eagerness, 77–78
Ekman, Paul, 83–85, 100, 109
emblems, 32, 89–90. *See also* gestures
emotions
  baseline readings for, 93–94, 104
  body language and, 72–75
  breathing and, 76–77
  charisma and, 48, 59–61
  in communication, 111–112
  compelling nature of, 61–63
  constellations of body language in,
    92–93
  contagiousness of, 110–115
  controlling, 65–68
  decision making and ability to
    process, 16
  energy levels and, 157–158
  gestures and, 11, 29–31
  influence and, 152–153
  love, 30–31
  method acting, 56–59
  in micro-expressions, 85–88
  mirror neurons and, 62–64

mistakes in projecting, 55–56
passion, 67
premeeting ritual for, 68–70, 76–77
projecting, 9, 10, 53–82
in public speaking, 199
reactive, 66
reading others', 10–11, 83–118
self-assessment of control of, 72–74
self-awareness of, 47–48
showing, 142, 159–161
in virtual communication, 164–165
voice frequencies and, 123–124,
   133–134, 142
empathy, 62–63, 64–65, 110–115
emphasis, 146
End of Big, The (Mele), 234
energy levels, 146, 147, 148–149,
   157–158
expertise, 153
eyebrows, 97
eye contact, 80–81, 100–101, 102

Facial Action Coding System
   (FACS), 85
facial expressions
   of friend versus foe, 97–98
   lying and, 84–85
   micro-expressions, 85–87, 91,
      109–110
   power and, 77–78
fears, 13, 189–191
   breathing and, 76–77
   public speaking, 45–46, 197–198
   self-talk and, 71–72
Fiesole amphitheater, 231–232
focus, charismatic nature of, 60–61
foot movements, 95, 101, 136, 184–185
Forster, E. M., 3
framing, 223–224, 226–227
French Resistance, 122
friend versus foe evaluations, 32,
   92–93, 97–98, 107–109

Gershon, Michael, 179–180
gestures, 9, 16, 23–43

cognitive load and, 37–38
creating alignment with, 117
emblems, 32, 89–90
emotional content of, 94–95
emotional control and, 65–68
emotional focus through, 69–70
emotions conveyed through, 11
handshakes, 26–27
Harvard experiment with, 38–40
importance of in communication,
   28–30, 33–34, 35–42
"Jesus gesture," 38–40
love expressed through, 30–31
lying and, 101
meaning conveyed through, 32–33,
   36–38
mood indicated by, 105–106
"penguin gesture," 69–70
primacy of, 28–29
research on, 35–38
spoken word versus, 36–37, 40
thought determined by, 40–43
Goldin-Meadow, Susan, 35–38, 40–41
Gregory, Stanford, 122–126, 133–134
group dynamics, 17
groupthink, 111
gut responses, 16, 114–115, 175–200
   changing your beliefs and, 192–194
   chi and, 179–181
   external validation of, 194–196
   fears and, 189–192
   lies and, 101
   mastering, 186–189
   neurons in, 178–179
   personal history and, 182–183
   positive self-talk and, 191–192
   research on, 175–176
   sabotage by, 181–182
   training, 185–186
   uncontrolled, cost of, 182–185

handshakes, 26–27, 103–104
happiness, 17
Hasson, Uri, 201–202, 204
head positions, 78, 101, 102
Herbert, Frank, 120

Hero with a Thousand Faces, The (Campbell), 212
hierarchy of needs, 209–210
Hitchcock, Alfred, 218
honest signals, 12, 145–174
   activity, 146, 147, 148–149, 157–158
   consistency, 147, 149–150, 158–159
   in cyberspace, 161–166
   influence, 147–148, 152–154
   mimicry, 146, 147, 148, 154–157
   in public speaking, 167–173
   turning into power cues, 150–152
Horace, 223
hormones, 58–59
humor, 221
Hunger Games, The (Collins), 220

ideas, 209
"I Have a Dream" (King), 25, 135, 142
influence, 147–148, 152–154
information overload, 26, 91, 209, 223, 243
intent, 90
intimate space, 79, 80
intuition, 46–47, 48, 106–107, 109–110, 114–115. *See also* gut responses

"Jesus gesture," 38–40

Kalkhoff, Will, 125
King, Martin Luther, Jr., 25, 135, 142

Larry King Live, 122–124
leaders and leadership
   acquiring, 126, 134
   authenticity of, 14
   body language in, 5–6
   communication style and, 240–242
   conversation by, 138–140
   creating alignment in, 115–117
   desire for, 17–21
   empathy and, 65
   gestures and, 41–42
   honest signals and, 145–174

listening and, 242–244
   manipulation versus, 18
   pace of, 42
   preparedness of, 236–237
   selecting, 124–126
   self-assessment of, 48
   showing emotion by, 159–161
   storytelling and, 13–14, 207
   voice of, 11–12, 119–143
learning styles, 25–26
leg movements, 95, 101
lies and lying, recognizing, 84–85, 92–93, 100–101, 107–109
Lie to Me (TV show), 85
listening, 101–103, 105–106, 158, 242–244
Literary Mind, The (Turner), 208–209
logical thinking, 33–34, 125
love, gestures in expression of, 30–31
love stories, 212–213

manipulation, 18
   emotional control and, 65–68
   mastery versus, 22
mantras, 191–196
Maslow, Abraham, 209–210
mastery, 53–82
   charisma and, 48
   of emotions, 65–68
   of gut responses, 186–189
   influence and, 153–154
   manipulation versus, 22
   time required for, 14–15
   value of, 20–21
Maurice (Forster), 3
maximum resonance point (MRP), 131–134, 140–141
McCain, John, 125–126
McCloud, David, 150–151
meaning
   gestures in conveying, 32–33, 36–38
   storytelling and, 214
Medina, John, 162, 164
meetings
   eye contact in, 80–81
   premeeting ritual for, 68–70, 76–77

space zone management in, 79–80
virtual, honest signals in, 161–166
Mele, Nicco, 234
mental maps, 13, 71–72, 175–200
changing, 191–199
method acting, 56–59
mimicry, 146, 147, 148, 154–157
mirroring
building alignment with, 116
honest signal, 154–157
as honest signal, 146, 147, 148
low-frequency sounds, 123, 124
posture, alignment and, 98–99
mirror neurons, 16
emotions and, 62–63, 64–68
in public speaking, 170–171
synchronization of brain waves
and, 203
Morgan, Nick
Dalai Lama and, 1–3
father's sexual orientation, 3–4
success record of, 20
toboggan accident, 4–6
"Mr. Spock Theory of the Brain,"
33–34, 63–64
multitasking, 25–26
Muskie, Ed, 159, 160

nasal voices, 141
need, creating, 209–210
nervousness
audience perception of, 112
breathing and, 141
offstage beats and, 68–69
projecting, 55
in public speaking, 45–46, 71–72
recognizing/controlling, 187–189
neurons
distribution of, 16
mirror, 16, 62–68, 170–171, 203
neuroscience
of communication, 15–17
of emotions, 62–63
of gestures, 35–38
gestures and, 33–34
of gut responses, 178–179

of power cues, 8–9
of synchronization of brain waves,
13–14, 201–205
of visual input, 6–7
nodding, 97–98
nonverbal communication. See also
body language; gestures
emotional focus and, 72–75
evaluating understanding of,
46–47
mastering your, 53–82
mastery of, influence and,
153–154
projecting charisma in, 10
reading others', 10–11, 83–118
research on, 15–17
self-awareness of, 9
showing confidence with, 16
simultaneous conversations with,
27–30
time for mastery of, 14–15
value of mastering, 20–21

Obama, Barack, 125–126
offstage beats, 68–70
Olivier, Laurence, 241
openness
consistency and, 159
eyes and eyebrows indicating, 97
gestures and, 38–40, 94–95
"penguin gesture" and, 69–70
in public speaking, 197
Orton, Peter, 206

passion, 67, 152–153
pecking order, 134
"penguin gesture," 69–70
Penn and Teller, 184–185
Pentland, Sandy, 145–147, 149,
156, 157
performance anxiety, 45–46
persistence, 235–240
persona, projecting your desired, 10,
53–82
personal space, 79, 80, 169–170, 171

persuasion, 140
    consistency and, 159
    posture and, 98–99
    storytelling in, 209–221
phobias, 13
phone conversations, 123–124
pitches, success in, 12, 156–157
poker, 94–95
positive self-talk, 191–194
    external validation of, 194–196
    for public speaking prep, 196–199
posture, 26–27
    charisma and, 59
    in listening, 102
    mirroring, 98–99, 116
    of power, 96
    power communicated through,
        77–79
    voice and, 142
power
    acquiring, 96
    body language of, 92–93, 95–97
    low-frequency sounds and, 16, 120,
        121–126
    posture and, 77–79
    questions to determine, 107–109
    recognizing/picking sides with,
        124–126
    taking control of, 8–9
power cues, 9–14
    honest signals, 12, 145–174
    projecting emotions/persona, 10,
        53–82
    reading others, 10–11, 83–118
    self-awareness, 9, 23–51
    storytelling, 13–14, 201–229
    unconscious story lines, 13,
        175–200
    voice, 11–12, 119–143
PowerPoint, 25–26, 168–169
presence, 41, 43–45, 137–138, 233–234.
        See also charisma
    emotional control and, 66–68
    voice in, 141–142
Presence (Rodenburg), 137–138
presidents, voices of US, 125–126,
        132–133

public speaking. *See also* storytelling
    audience involvement in, 224,
        227–228
    beginning, 221–223
    creating trust and credibility in,
        18–19
    emotions in, 199
    engaging audience interest in,
        169–173
    eye contact in, 80–81
    fear of, 45–46
    focus on audience in, 72
    gestures and openness in, 38–40
    honest signals in, 167–173
    misconceptions about, 24–25
    positive self-talk for, 196–199
    PowerPoint and, 25–26
    preparedness for, 112, 167, 198,
        233–240
    projecting charisma in, 70–72
    room layouts and, 171–173
    verbal tics and, 135–137
public zone, 79

Quayle, Dan, 124
questions
    phrasing as polarities, 107–110
    phrasing to your unconscious,
        11, 114
quest stories, 211–212, 224

radical connectivity, 234–244
rags-to-riches stories, 213
rational thinking, 33–34, 125
Reagan, Ronald, 132–133
reasons, 209
repetition, 24–25
requests, 209
revenge stories, 213
rhetoric, 232, 241
Right to Speak, The (Rodenburg),
        137–138
Rizzolatti, Giacomo, 62–63
Robb, Chuck, 150–151
Rodenburg, Patsy, 137–138

Index

safety, 17, 18–19
salary reviews, 57–59
sales, 12, 156–157
Second Brain, The (Gershon), 179–180
self-awareness, 9
  of body language, 43–46
  body language diary for, 43–45
  of charisma levels, 47–48
  cognitive load of maintaining,
    54–55
  developing, 42
  of gestures, 23–43
  of honest signals, 150
  of intuition level, 46–47
  inventory in, 42
  of posture, 26–27
  questionnaire on, 49–50
  of unconscious behavior, 34–35
  of verbal tics, 136–137
self-destructive behaviors, 185–186
self-protection, 71–72, 197–198
self-talk, 71–72, 191–194
  positive, 191–196
serotonin, 180–181
signaling mechanisms, 146. *See also*
  honest signals
singing, 133–134
smiling, 77–78, 97–98, 123–124
social cues, 162–163
social relations, 145–147
social zone, 79
space zones, social, 79–80, 94, 95,
  169–173
standing ovations, 226–228
Stanislavski, Constantin, 56–57
Star Wars (movie), 219
Stewart, Jon, 96
stillness, 96
storytelling, 13–14, 201–229
  additional elements of great,
    217–227
  anecdotes versus, 206–207
  archetypes in, 210–214, 216–217,
    224–226
  beginnings in, 217–218, 221–223
  business stories, 221–226

  character development in, 221
  conflict in, 220
  details in, 219
  framing in, 223–224, 226–227
  love stories, 212–213
  morals in, 219–220
  need and, 209–210
  organization in, 214–217
  quest stories, 211–212
  rags-to-riches stories, 213
  revenge stories, 213
  standing ovations for, 226–228
  stranger in a strange land stories, 212
  surprises in, 218
  what it is, 208–221
  what it isn't, 206–208
stranger in a strange land stories, 212,
  225–226
success
  honest signals and, 12
  social signals and, 145–147
  voice and, 11–12
suggestions, 209
synchrony, 146

tact, 161
360-degree evaluations, 45
toboggan accident, 4–6
tone of voice. *See* voice
transparency, 236–237
Transportation Security
  Administration (TSA), 85
tribalism, 18–21, 242–243
trust, 100–101, 163, 165–166
truth versus lies, recognizing, 84–85,
  92–93, 100–101, 107–109. *See also*
  honest signals
Turner, Mark, 208–209

unconscious mind
  attention limitations and, 53–55
  control by, 6–8, 34–35
  emotion recognition in, 85–89
  gestures in shaping, 32–33

unconscious mind (*continued*)
harnessing expertise of, 105–106
intuition and, 106–107
listening to, 109–110, 114
mastering, 187–189
mental maps in, 182–183
positive self-talk and, 191–194
power relationships and, 8–9
reading others', 10–11
self-talk of, 13, 71–72
shaping questions to, 11, 107–109
speed of compared with conscious
thought, 31
system for polling, 113–114
tapping into expertise of, 90–93
training, 185–186

verbal tics, 135–137
virtual communication, 161–166
visual input, 6–7, 25
visualization, 186
vocoders, 122–123
voice, 11–12, 119–143
authoritative arc in, 134–135
breath control and, 128–130, 141
charisma and, 137–138
deep, advantages of, 126–128
developing, 127–128
emotions and, 123–124, 133–134
honest signals and, 12
low-frequency sounds in, 16, 120,
121–126
lying and, 101
maintaining, 140–143
maximum resonance point in,
131–134, 140–141
nasal, 141–142
overtones/undertones in, 121,
126–127
tension in, 130–131
of US presidents, 125–126, 132–133
verbal tics, 135–137

Watzke, Heribert, 178
Webster, Stephen, 122–126
wish fulfillment, 108–109

ACKNOWLEDGMENTS

This book has had a long gestation. Thanks are due to Esmond Harmsworth, agent extraordinaire and patient midwife for helping me at every stage of the birthing process.

Once again, I'm delighted to be working with Jeff Kehoe and the team at Harvard Business Review Press. I deeply appreciate Jeff's patience and ability to discern the outlines of a book when the idea was a little hazier in its early days.

Many clients and friends have helped by fearlessly trying out these ideas in various ways and helping me develop them, sometimes in front of live audiences. Jeff Johnson was an early and clear-eyed reader, and I am deeply grateful for his help. David Meerman Scott, Josh Linkner, Peter Orton, Vince Molinaro, Liane Davey, Nicco Mele, Rick Chavez, Lisa Schilling, Adam Hartung, Pam Slim, Alex Kinnier, Amy Martin, Chris Brogan, David Pollay, Doc Searls, Frank Rose, Les Gold, Jordan Broad, Sam Weston and the folks at HUGE, Glenn Llopis, Jill Burch, Kaihan Krippendorff, Lisa Merlo-Booth, Majka Burhardt, Mark Sanborn, Sally Hogshead, Nick Vitalari, Micah Solomon, Nancy Goldman, Lesley Bakker, Rob Coneybeer, Ruth Mott, Soren Kaplan, Sue Ershler, Tim Sanders, Tim Washer, and the Air Force Special Ops Team all helped me with their intelligence, practice, and commitment.

The Public Words team is tops on the honor roll in so many ways for helping develop these ideas over the years and contributing their thoughts, energy, brilliance, and love. Thanks, Nikki, Emma, and Sarah.

ACKNOWLEDGMENTS

Thanks particularly to Sarah, who helped immeasurably with a brilliant edit of the rough draft to knock it into shape. I am blessed.

Thanks once again to my wonderful family, now in three countries and five cities, for all the love, help, and listening, spoken and unspoken. Thanks, Nikki, Emma and Dave, Sarah and Jack, Eric and Julia, Howard and Rita.

Finally, all my love and gratitude to my wife, Nikki, who has listened to these ideas in various stages more times than anyone should have to in one lifetime. Thanks for the suggestions, discussions, and hugs. You rock.

ABOUT THE AUTHOR

NICK MORGAN is one of America's top communication theorists and coaches. He works with professional speakers, executives, celebrities, and organizations to help them shape ideas and make them irresistible to an impatient, information-saturated world.

A passionate teacher, Nick is committed to helping people find clarity in their thinking and ideas—and then delivering them with panache. He has been commissioned by Fortune 50 companies to write for many CEOs and presidents. He has coached people to give congressional testimony, to appear on the *Today Show*, and to address the investment community. He has worked widely with political and educational leaders. And he has helped design conferences and prepare keynote speeches around the world.

He's also a speaker to global audiences on subjects relating to communications, including storytelling, body language, and persuasion.

Nick's methods, which are well known for challenging conventional thinking, have been published worldwide. His most recent book is *Trust Me: Four Steps to Authenticity and Charisma*, published in December 2008 by Jossey-Bass. His acclaimed book on public speaking, *Working the Room: How to Move People to Action through Audience-Centered Speaking*, was published by Harvard Business School Press in 2003 and reprinted in paperback in 2005 as *Give Your Speech, Change the World: How to Move Your Audience to Action*. In addition,

Nick has published almost a dozen ebooks, as well as chapters in other people's books.

Nick served as editor of the *Harvard Management Communication Letter* from 1998 to 2003. He has written hundreds of articles for local and national publications. Nick is a former fellow at the Center for Public Leadership at the Harvard Kennedy School.

After earning his PhD in literature and rhetoric, Nick spent a number of years teaching courses on Shakespeare and public speaking at the University of Virginia and Princeton University. He wrote speeches for Virginia Governor Charles S. Robb and went on to found his own communications consulting organization, Public Words, in 1997.

Nick hikes and cycles in his spare time, and bangs out the occasional tune on the piano and classical guitar.